UPPARK

West Sussex

THE NATIONAL TRUST

ACKNOWLEDGEMENTS

In the rescue and repair of Uppark, the Trust has incurred many debts: to those who fought the fire or rescued contents; to the workers who retrieved fragments from the ruins; to the conservators for emergency and subsequent work; to the architects, contractors, builders and craftsmen who designed or carried out the repairs. The Trust is also grateful to English Heritage for providing the services of its archaeological team and to HM The Queen and the Royal Collection Trust for providing help with emergency picture conservation after the fire. Sun Alliance, which, as the Sun Fire Office, first insured Uppark in 1753, has worked closely with the Trust and sponsored the Sun Alliance Exhibition & Visitor Centre as well as various Uppark publications. The exhibition chronicles the restoration of Uppark from the fire on 30 August 1989 through to its reopening on 1 June 1995.

For help with this book, I am indebted to the Meade-Fetherstonhaugh family for permission to consult and publish documents in their possession, and to Timothy McCann, who administers the family archive loaned to the West Sussex Record Office. John Eyre has kindly made available his transcripts of papers destroyed in the fire and has made many helpful comments on the text. Anthony du Boulay, Hon. Adviser on Ceramics to the National Trust, wrote the entries on the porcelain. Oliver Garnett, the Trust's Guidebook Editor, drew up the lists of pictures, from notes compiled by St. John Gore and Alastair Laing. Tracey Avery and Nino Strachey undertook most of the research. I am also grateful to Conall MacFarlane and to his colleagues at Christie's (in particular to Dr Timothy Hunter) for advice on aspects of the collection. Thanks are also due to Fred Aldsworth, Dr Peter Brears, Stephen Calloway, Thomas Campbell, Antony Cleminson, Margaret Davidson, Dorothy Edwards, Catherine Hassall, Iain McLaren, Barbara Megson, Hans Meier, Martin Mortimer, Marigold Webb, Jeremy Wood and Lavinia Wellicome.

Christopher Rowell

Photographs: British Architectural Library, RIBA, London pp. 12, 18; Country Life Picture Library p. 85; English Heritage p. 11; P. Fagan p. 41; National Trust pp. 8, 32, 33, 88; National Trust Photographic Library pp. 31, 34, 35, 37, 54; NTPL/Matthew Antrobus p. 47; NTPL/ Prudence Cuming p. 27; NTPL/Andreas von Einsiedel pp. 19, 23, 44, 45, 51, 53, 55, 56, 61, 62, 65, 67, 69, 75, 77, back cover; NTPL/Geoffrey Frosh pp. 50, 81; NTPL/John Hammond front cover, pp. 9, 14, 16, 17, 21, 25, 70, 87; NTPL/Angelo Hornak pp. 22, 72; NTPL/Christopher Hurst p. 76; NTPL/Nadia MacKenzie pp. 4, 59, 64; NTPL/Sheila Orme p. 83; NTPL/James Pipkin p. 66; NTPL/Tim Stephens pp. 7, 43, 91, 93; NTPL/Rupert Truman p. 42; NTPL/ J. Whitaker pp. 78; The News, Portsmouth p. 40; Ian West p. 39; West Sussex County Record Office p. 79; WSCRO/John Hammond pp. 1, 28, 89.

First published in Great Britain in 1995 by the National Trust
© 1995 The National Trust; reprinted 1995; reprinted with corrections 1996
Registered charity no. 205846

ISBN 0 7078 0198 2

Designed by James Shurmer

Phototypeset in Monotype Bembo Series 270
by Southern Positives and Negatives (SPAN), Lingfield, Surrey (T022)

Printed in Great Britain by Balding + Mansell
for National Trust Enterprises Ltd, 36 Queen Anne's Gate, London SW1H 9AS

(*Front cover*) Uppark from the south-west in the early eighteenth century; detail from the painting by Pieter Tillemans (Staircase Hall)

(*Title-page*) Uppark from the south, from Repton's Red Book of 1810

(*Back cover*) The stained-glass window in the Servery, c.1813

CONTENTS

FOREWORD

Although Uppark was donated to the National Trust by our father and grandfather in 1954, it has always remained our family home.

Our first memories of Uppark are of staying there with our grandparents, which we all had mixed feelings about – albeit awesome, exciting and entertaining. We remember being shown the doll's-house upstairs before going to bed, when often we ended up huddled together in a four-poster bed. Other memories at that age are of the grandeur and size of the place, along with the ferocity of the Scottish housekeeper, who kept the servants and ourselves in order.

Uppark became our home in 1968, when our mother, Jean Meade-Fetherstonhaugh, moved in with us three girls. Her challenge as Richard's widow was to make it a home in as practical a way as possible, and through her hard work, knowledge and good taste she made this happen.

From this time on, Uppark played a very important part in all our lives. In 1972 the first of the next generation arrived, followed by a further six, the youngest born only three weeks before the fire. They were the first small children to live at Uppark, creating a lively and happy family environment. The house certainly lent itself to parties, and we will especially remember the wonderful Christmases there, with the huge tree, brought in off the estate, reaching the ceiling of the Stone Hall and all lit with candles. We were all married from the house, the Red Drawing Room and our Drawing Room upstairs being used for the Blessings.

The three of us live on the estate with our husbands and children, and we continue to manage, maintain and farm the land which our father loved so much; we feel he would be proud to know of our commitment.

Moving back into Uppark will create a challenging task for us all. The restoration now complete, a new life begins. We all feel that the special atmosphere at Uppark was created by Lady Sarah Fetherstonhaugh, the memory of which we will have for ever.

Harriet de Bianchi Cossart   Emma Goad   Sophie Warre

(Opposite page) The Little Parlour

INTRODUCTION

On 30 August 1989 Uppark was severely damaged by fire. Its repair has been the most complicated the National Trust has ever undertaken. Uppark re-opened its doors in the Trust's centenary year, a timely celebration of British conservation skills.

If there is much that has been learned and to be grateful for since the fire, there is continuing sorrow for what has been lost. The Meade-Fetherstonhaugh family's possessions were totally destroyed. The loss of the private rooms and their contents on the upper floors removed from Uppark an intrinsic element of its fame as a house unaltered since the nineteenth century. Downstairs, the patina of age has largely gone from several rooms, but it was possible to preserve much of the old paint and gilding, untouched since c.1815, in the Saloon and Dining Room. The aim has been to restore Uppark, 'in so far as that is practicable', to its state before the fire. Old and new have been carefully interwoven and recorded, but it is hoped that their junction is invisible and that a seamless repair has been achieved.

Sir William Ford, whose family bought the estate between 1549 and 1560, was living in a house at Uppark by 1595. This building, about which very little is known, was pulled down and rebuilt around 1690, probably by William Talman, for Ford, 3rd Lord Grey of Warke. Grey was both Uppark's most important and most unscrupulous inhabitant. Convicted of treason for his involvement in Monmouth's Rebellion in 1685, he narrowly escaped execution. Later he attained high office under William III, who created him Earl of Tankerville.

From the outside, Uppark looks much as it did in Tankerville's day, although the interior was extensively remodelled by Sir Matthew Fetherstonhaugh, who bought the estate in 1747. Sir Matthew, who came of a landed and mercantile Northumbrian family, inherited £400,000 from a kinsman in 1746. He acquired a wife and a baronetcy soon afterwards, and probably employed James Paine to embellish his new country seat. During a two-year Grand Tour, Sir Matthew bought pictures and furniture for Uppark, and also perhaps, for his London house in Whitehall, which was built by James Paine between 1754 and 1758. Sir Matthew was a man of parts: landowner, speculator, politician, collector, patron, scientist, philanthropist and gambler. His only son, Sir Harry, is famous for his brief liaison with the young Emma Hamilton, for his friendship with the Prince Regent, and for his marriage in 1825, when over 70, to his 20-year-old dairy maid. A francophile, he acquired French furniture, porcelain and fittings for rooms constructed or redecorated by Humphry Repton, who also improved the garden and park.

Sir Harry's estate was inherited in 1846 by his widow, Mary Ann, and in 1875 by her sister, Frances, who assumed the Fetherstonhaugh name on inheriting Uppark. By tradition, they preserved the house unchanged in pious tribute to Sir Harry's memory, but in reality they made normal household improvements. In 1895, in default of a suitable Fetherstonhaugh heir, Frances Fetherstonhaugh bequeathed Uppark to the younger son of the 4th Earl and Countess Winterton, friends at Shillinglee Park. On Colonel Keith Turnour-Fetherstonhaugh's death in 1930, the bequest passed to Admiral Sir Herbert Meade, younger son of the 4th Earl and Countess of Clanwilliam, also former Sussex friends of the Fetherstonhaugh sisters. The Admiral's wife, Lady Meade-Fetherstonhaugh, fell in love with Uppark, finding her vocation in its careful restoration. In a pioneering decade of textile conservation in the 1930s, she ensured that the essence of Uppark was passed on in a sound condition. In 1954 Uppark was given to the National Trust by the Admiral and his eldest son, Richard.

The Saloon after the fire

CHAPTER ONE
EARLY HISTORY

'Up Park': the site explains the old spelling – parkland high on the West Sussex Downs looking south over a broad valley to the Solent and the Isle of Wight. There has been a house here since at least 1595, when the county maps first noted a building within the park pale. Previously, the owners of the estate lived at Harting Place, which stood next to South Harting church. This was the stronghold of the Hussey family, who owned Harting from 1115 to 1549. Licence to fortify and crenellate was granted by Henry III in 1266. A park was created before 1274 and was stocked with deer in 1332. In 1370 a valuation of Henry Hussey's estate mentioned 'the Park on the Down' and 'A certain park

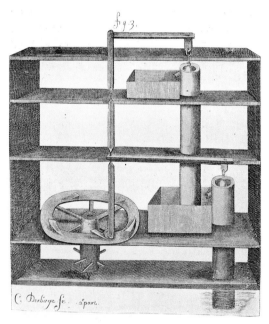

Edward Ford's water pump; engraving by C. Derbaye from 'Journal des Voyages de Monsieur de Monconys' (1666)

called Le Upparke, with pasture and wood'. By this time, two-thirds of the cleared land was pasture, the remainder arable, but most of the estate was still heavily wooded. In 1349 there were several sheep farms and by 1440 Up Parke and Down Parke were leased to Robert Legge, a London draper. The price of wool increased considerably between 1515 and 1531, and fine Southdown fleeces were exported to Spain from nearby Portsmouth. This was probably the attraction of the Harting estate to Edmund Ford, the son of a Devon wool merchant, who purchased the main portion for £1,600 in 1549. By 1560 he had bought additional parts of the old Hussey lands for £1,800. These large sums were justified by the value not only of the sheep and timber, but also of the iron forges at West Harting and Nyewood.

On Edmund's death in 1568, the estate was inherited by his two daughters, Magdalen and Dorothy, who divided it in 1582. It was after this division that the first house was built at Uppark. The builder may have been Magdalen's son, Sir William Ford (b.1571), a Royalist during the Civil War, who on 24 October 1645 complained to Parliament about the Chichester Puritans who had 'caused many of yr. Petitioner's trees to be cut downe close about his house which standeth upon a hill', and had seized furniture, stock and goods.

In 1641 Sir William's son, Sir Edward Ford (1605–70), soldier, engineer and inventor, vowed to raise for the King 'a thousand men and to undertake the conquest of Sussex'. Knighted in 1643, Sir Edward was besieged at Arundel Castle, which, as owner of Uppark, he had an ancient feudal duty to defend. According to Clarendon, his eventual defeat was partly due to his lack of military experience, despite his 'honour and courage'. Imprisoned in the Tower, he retired to the Continent on his release. On suspicion of 'being privy to the King's escape from Hampton Court' in 1647, a third

The view from Uppark down to South Harting. By the pond is the Engine House from which water was pumped up to the house; painting by Joseph Francis Gilbert, 1834 (Tapestry Bedroom)

of his estate was confiscated, but he soon had a proportion of the fine remitted. That his wife was Sarah Ireton, sister of the Parliamentary general, may have helped. In 1656, during the Protectorate, with Cromwell's encouragement, Sir Edward was requested by the City of London to devise a method of pumping water 93 feet from the Thames to the highest streets. This he accomplished in one year at his own expense. The same 'rare engine' was subsequently used elsewhere to drain mines and farmland. In partnership with Thomas Toogood, he later obtained a royal licence to erect waterworks in several London districts. Ford is traditionally credited with the feat of pumping water up from South Harting to Uppark, but the height (at 310 feet) was well beyond the ingenuity of seventeenth-century engineers. Uppark must have depended on wells and dew ponds until before 1746, when a

water supply had been 'sometime since erected' by means of lead pipes and 'an engine in the South Gardens at the base of the South Harting hills' (presumably within the Engine House that still stands on the edge of South Harting village). Maintenance of a 'Water Engine' is mentioned in the accounts of 1731.

After the Restoration of Charles II in 1660, Sir Edward turned his mind to the improvement of coinage, the overhaul of the navy and the encouragement of trade. He died in 1670 while in Ireland supervising the machinery he had patented for minting farthings.

CHAPTER TWO
THE TANKERVILLE HOUSE

Uppark was inherited by Sir Edward Ford's daughter, Catherine (1634–c.1682), who married secondly Ralph, 2nd Lord Grey of Warke (1630–75), of a Northumberland family seated at Chillingham Castle, still famous for its ancient herd of wild white cattle. The peerage had been granted in 1624 to Ralph's father, Sir William Grey, a Parliamentarian during the Civil War and a member of Cromwell's Council of State. It was the 1st Lord Grey's grandson, Ford Grey (1655–1701), who rebuilt Uppark around 1690.

Ford, 3rd Lord Grey of Warke, Viscount Glendale and Earl of Tankerville, was a more colourful character than the sober restraint of Uppark would suggest. He was both its most important and its most unscrupulous inhabitant. In an age of flexible principles, Grey was notorious for his duplicity. His political abilities and influence were great; he had considerable oratorical powers. In 1681, as a Protestant Whig, he was prominent among the advocates of the bill to exclude the Catholic Duke of York (the future James II) from the succession. His private life was unconventional. Having married Mary, daughter of the 1st Earl of Berkeley, he eloped with her sister, Henrietta. In 1682 he was brought to trial by her outraged father for 'conspiring, contriving, practising, and intending the final ruin of the lady Henrietta Berkeley', but although convicted, got off on a technicality. In 1683 a riot involving the Lord Mayor of London resulted in a large fine.

At this time Grey was deeply involved in the treasonable anti-Catholic plotting of the Duke of Monmouth, the illegitimate son of Charles II, whose first attempt to usurp the throne resulted in the Rye House Plot (1683) to kidnap and assassinate the King. Uppark was intended as a haven for Monmouth until the ensuing rebellion. When the conspiracy was detected, Grey was arrested, but while he was being taken to the Tower, he offered the sergeant-at-arms, Mr Deerham, a drink. After fourteen bottles of claret, Deerham was, not surprisingly, incapable of preventing Grey's escape. In disguise Grey rode to Uppark and then with his mistress took ship from Chichester for Flushing.

During Monmouth's campaign against James II in 1685, Grey was the Duke's principal lieutenant, but was an ineffectual military commander. Monmouth proclaimed himself King of England on 20 June, but his claim melted away at Sedgemoor (5 and 6 July), where his Taunton infantry held their ground, but the cavalry (under Grey's command), 'being newly raised and undisciplin'd', was easily dispersed by the Government troops. Monmouth and Grey fled the field, but were soon captured.

Monmouth was executed, but Grey preserved his life by testifying against his former adherents (on condition that no one should die upon his evidence). He also gave a bond for the huge sum of £40,000 to the Lord President of the Council, the 1st Earl of Rochester, and financial promises to other courtiers. In 1687 Evelyn recorded that Rochester was to receive '£1700 per Ann for ever out of Lord Grey's Estate'. In June 1686 Grey was pardoned and his title and honours restored. This was a remarkable reprieve, due to the vast sum of money Grey could muster and his willingness to betray his friends. Grey lay low at Uppark until the invasion of William of Orange in 1688, when he supported the Dutch stadtholder's claim to the throne. After the coronation of William and Mary he took an active part in politics and in 1695 was made Privy Councillor and created Viscount Glendale and Earl of Tankerville. In 1696 he was appointed a Commissioner for Trade, First Commissioner of the Treasury (1699) and Lord Privy Seal (1700).

Dryden dismissed Grey in his satire *Absalom and Achitophel* (1681) as 'below the Dignity of Verse' and Bishop Burnet described him as a 'cowardly,

Ford, 1st Earl of Tankerville, the builder of Uppark; by Peter Lely
(Audley End, Essex; by kind permission of The Lord Braybrooke)

perfidious person', but it is unlikely that the intelligent and able William III would have placed much trust in him had he been devoid of ability and acumen. Grey took huge risks and was guilty of high treason, but his adherence to Protestantism, the Whig party and Parliamentary government appears to have been genuine.

Given the circumstances of Ford Grey's extraordinary career, Uppark must have been erected after the Glorious Revolution of 1688 and before the traveller and diarist Celia Fiennes described it as 'new built' in 1695, the year that Grey was created Earl of Tankerville. The engraving of Uppark published in *Britannia Illustrata* (1707) accords with Celia Fiennes's description: 'Square, with nine windows in the front and seven in the sides, brickwork with free stone coynes and windows, in the midst of fine gardens, gravell and grass walks and bowling green . . .'. As today, the woodland was opened up southwards to take advantage of the majestic view across the Downs towards the Solent. The approach was from the east via two courtyards, the outer flanked by stable and service blocks.

Uppark is one of the finest surviving examples within a tradition of country house building introduced to England from Holland in the 1660s by gentleman-architects like Hugh May and Roger Pratt. Symmetry and simplicity are its hallmarks, and Uppark shares many of its other common features: a hipped roof with a deep cornice, dormer windows and tall chimneystacks; a central three-bay frontispiece set slightly forward, with a pediment which once contained the Grey coat of arms (later replaced by the Fetherstonhaughs'); two principal

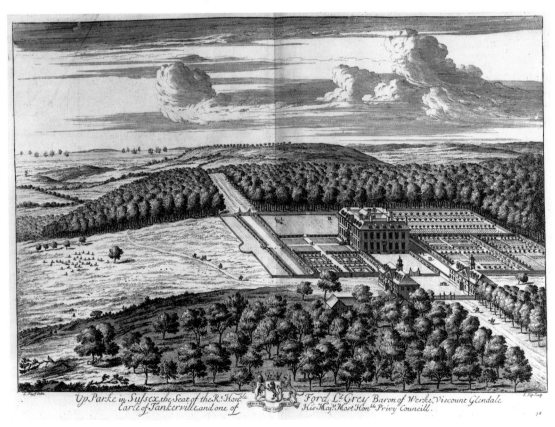

Lord Tankerville's house and formal gardens, as they were drawn by Leonard Knyff and engraved by Johannes Kip in 1695–1701. The engraving was published in 'Britannia Illustrata' (1707)

floors separated by a plain string course, above a semi-basement; and steps up to a pedimented doorway on the south front leading into the principal room on the principal floor (although at Uppark the day-to-day entrance was then on the east side of the house). Uppark is reminiscent of May's elegant domestic style, markedly Dutch in its use of brick with stone dressings, and though not vernacular, simpler than the more formal classicism of Inigo Jones and Pratt.

As for the architect, James Dallaway's attribution (1815) to William Talman is credible, even though his documented *oeuvre* is small and eclectic. Dallaway's assertion, does, however, need to be treated with caution, given that he ascribed Humphry Repton's contemporary alterations at Uppark to his rival John Nash. The recent discovery that Talman probably designed the future Duke of Marlborough's Holywell House, St Albans, Hertfordshire (1686), shows that he could work in the plain Anglo-Dutch idiom of Uppark. Dallaway also credited Talman with the contemporary and virtually identical (though now much altered) Stansted Park, the Sussex seat of his former captor, Richard, Viscount Lumley, later 1st Earl of Scarbrough. Lumley had been a Catholic and Treasurer to Charles II's queen, Catherine of Braganza, but later adopted the Protestant cause. Like Ford Grey, he was rewarded for his political support by William III, whom Talman served from 1689 as Comptroller of Works – in the alteration of Hampton Court Palace, for example.

The earliest comprehensive inventories of Uppark (dated 1705 and 1722) reveal that the ground plan has remained essentially unchanged. The Little Parlour and Stone Hall have even retained their original names. On the principal floor, ranges of apartments along the east and west fronts flank two much larger rooms, which form the spine of the house – the Staircase Hall and what was then a formal entrance hall called the Great, or Marble, Hall (now Saloon). The sequence of flanking rooms moved from the public domain of the Great and Little Parlours at the south-west and south-east corners of the house to the privacy of bedchambers and closets at the north-west and north-east.

The principal rooms on the ground and first floors were panelled or hung with gilt leather, tapestry or woven textiles. Although the ground-floor rooms were subsequently remodelled, much of the painted bolection panelling survived intact elsewhere until the fire. Even the seventeenth-century Brussels tapestries in the first-floor Prince Regent's Bedroom (in 1705, possibly the 'Roome hangd with forest Tapestrey') had survived. After the fire, sections of the panelling and balustrade of the Staircase are all that remain of the seventeenth-century woodwork (although the fire revealed panelling beneath subsequent wallpaper in the Little Parlour). The mid-eighteenth-century and later remodelling also moved doors and fireplaces, and it is now clear that Lord Tankerville's Great Hall originally rose the full height of the house (a mezzanine floor incorporating the Print Room and two flanking rooms was inserted when the Saloon was constructed *c.*1770).

Lord Tankerville's only child, Mary (d.1710), inherited Uppark on his death in 1701. In 1695 she had married Charles Bennet, 2nd Lord Ossulston (*c.*1674–1722), who, in 1714 was made 1st Earl of Tankerville of the second creation. Ossulston's father had been raised to the peerage in 1682, having been Deputy Postmaster (1666–72) and having 'left behind him a great estate'. In 1719–20 the new Lord Tankerville employed the French architect Nicholas Dubois, probably at his own family seat, Dawley House, Middlesex, which he was then enlarging or rebuilding. The sparseness of the furnishings at Uppark inventoried in 1722, the year of Lord Tankerville's death, suggests that he spent most of his time at Dawley, where he died.

Tankerville's son, also Charles, the 2nd Earl (1697–1753), was a soldier and courtier, holding among other Court posts, the Mastership of the Buckhounds (1733–7). The 2nd Earl seems to have been at Uppark more often than his father. He certainly valued it as a hunting-box, and had two views of the house and surrounding country by Pieter Tillemans installed in the panelling of the Staircase Hall. He commissioned a new stable (1723–5) from a London builder, John Jenner, who also made alterations to the Earl's London house in 1727. Comparison between Knyff and Kip's view of Uppark (1695–1701) and that by Tillemans (before

Uppark from the south-west before 1734; by Pieter Tillemans (Staircase Hall). The two service buildings beyond the house were demolished c.1750, when James Paine probably built the present pavilions flanking the house

1734) shows that pediments and dormer windows were removed from the pair of stable and service blocks to the east of the house. Recent excavations have revealed their foundations and the tunnel that linked the south block to the main house. After a furtive romance Lord Tankerville and his sixteen-year-old bride, Camilla Colville (1698–1775), the daughter of a Northumberland butcher and grazier, were married about 1715 at Jarrow. In 1737 she was appointed Lady of the Bedchamber to Queen Caroline, consort of George II. Lord Hervey described her as 'a handsome, good-natured, simple woman (to whom the King had formerly been *coquet*)'. Her husband also had his amours: in 1738 he was ill at Uppark, being nursed by his mistress.

Despite his undoubted wealth (Tankerville owned the second largest house in St James's Square), Uppark was sold in 1747 for £19,000 to Sir Matthew Fetherstonhaugh, whose family were seated at Fetherstonhaugh Castle, Northumberland. Tankerville owned estates in Northumberland, and had been Lord Lieutenant of the county since 1740, so this may have encouraged the sale to a Northumbrian family. The Fetherstonhaughs' Whig affiliations might also have been a recommendation. The matter was arranged by Tankerville's agent, William Battine, to whom he wrote with aristocratic insouciance: 'I don't know how to set about it myself being not only very ignorant in these affairs but likewise an exceeding indolent fellow'. The survey map signed and dated 1746 by James Crow, shows the extent of Sir Matthew's new acquisition, of which Uppark was the main part. The sale included the pumping house and engine, with lead pipes to draw water up to the house, and the timber in the park, which was assessed as equal to the £19,000 price of the estate. After acquiring Uppark, Sir Matthew maintained a connection with Lord Tankerville (his Account Book records a visit in 1749), and he employed Tankerville's agent, Battine, who became a family friend. Battine's son, also William, a lawyer, poet and Whig, was to have his bust by Garrard placed in the Whig Pantheon of Sir Harry Fetherstonhaugh's Dining Room.

THE OWNERS OF UPPARK

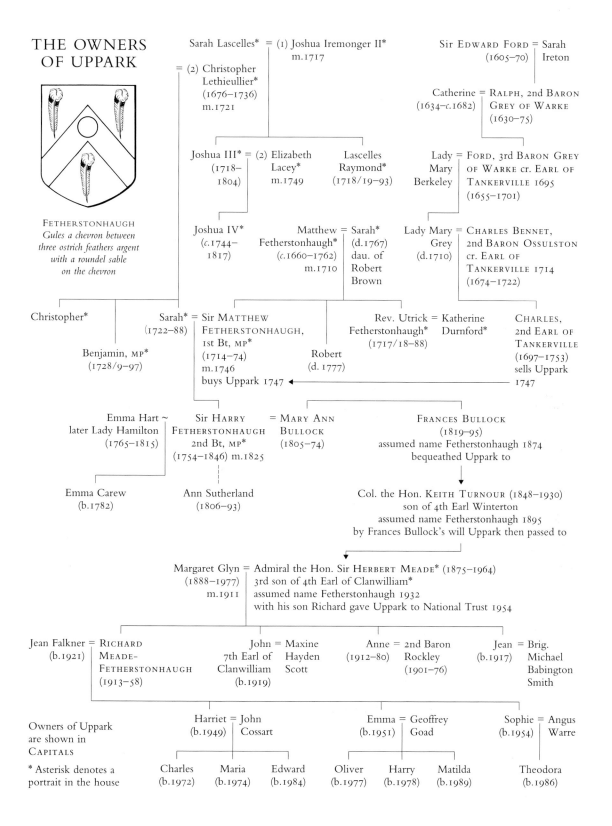

FETHERSTONHAUGH
*Gules a chevron between
three ostrich feathers argent
with a roundel sable
on the chevron*

Sarah Lascelles* = (1) Joshua Iremonger II*
                      m.1717

= (2) Christopher
Lethieullier*
(1676–1736)
m.1721

Sir EDWARD FORD = Sarah
(1605–70) | Ireton

Catherine = RALPH, 2nd BARON
(1634–c.1682) | GREY OF WARKE
                (1630–75)

Joshua III* = (2) Elizabeth   Lascelles   Lady = FORD, 3rd BARON GREY
(1718–   Lacey*   Raymond*   Mary   OF WARKE cr. EARL OF
1804)   m.1749   (1718/19–93)   Berkeley TANKERVILLE 1695
                                                            (1655–1701)

Joshua IV*   Matthew = Sarah*   Lady Mary = CHARLES BENNET,
(c.1744–   Fetherstonhaugh* (d.1767) Grey   2nd BARON OSSULSTON
1817)   (c.1660–1762) dau. of   (d.1710)   cr. EARL OF
                       m.1710   Robert   TANKERVILLE 1714
                                   Brown   (1674–1722)

Christopher*   Sarah* = Sir MATTHEW   Rev. Utrick = Katherine   CHARLES,
               (1722–88) FETHERSTONHAUGH,   Fetherstonhaugh* Durnford*   2nd EARL OF
                          1st Bt, MP*   (1717/18–88)   TANKERVILLE
    Benjamin, MP*   (1714–74)   Robert   (1697–1753)
    (1728/9–97)   m.1746   (d. 1777)   sells Uppark
                          buys Uppark 1747 ◄———————————————————————————————— 1747

Emma Hart ~   Sir HARRY   = MARY ANN   FRANCES BULLOCK
later Lady Hamilton FETHERSTONHAUGH BULLOCK   (1819–95)
(1765–1815)   2nd Bt, MP*   (1805–74)   assumed name Fetherstonhaugh 1874
                 (1754–1846) m.1825   bequeathed Uppark to
                          |
Emma Carew   Ann Sutherland   Col. the Hon. KEITH TURNOUR (1848–1930)
(b.1782)   (1806–93)   son of 4th Earl Winterton
                                                  assumed name Fetherstonhaugh 1895
                                                  by Frances Bullock's will Uppark then passed to

          Margaret Glyn = Admiral the Hon. Sir HERBERT MEADE* (1875–1964)
          (1888–1977) | 3rd son of 4th Earl of Clanwilliam*
          m.1911 | assumed name Fetherstonhaugh 1932
                      | with his son Richard gave Uppark to National Trust 1954

Jean Falkner = RICHARD   John = Maxine   Anne = 2nd Baron   Jean = Brig.
(b.1921)   MEADE-   7th Earl of Hayden (1912–80) Rockley (b.1917) Michael
               FETHERSTONHAUGH Clanwilliam Scott   (1901–76)   Babington
               (1913–58)   (b.1919)   Smith

Owners of Uppark   Harriet = John   Emma = Geoffrey   Sophie = Angus
are shown in   (b.1949) | Cossart   (b.1951) | Goad   (b.1954) | Warre
CAPITALS

* Asterisk denotes a   Charles   Maria   Edward   Oliver   Harry   Matilda   Theodora
portrait in the house (b.1972) (b.1974) (b.1984) (b.1977) (b.1978) (b.1989) (b.1986)

CHAPTER THREE

SIR MATTHEW AND SIR HARRY FETHERSTONHAUGH

Sir Matthew Fetherstonhaugh, Bt (1714–74) was the eldest son of another Matthew (*c*.1660–1762), who had purchased Fetherstonhaugh Castle, the ancient Northumbrian seat of the family, in 1711. Sir Matthew's father's wealth derived from the coal and wine trades and from his marriage in 1710 to Sarah Brown (d.1767), who upon the death of an only brother became heiress to a large fortune. Matthew Fetherstonhaugh the Elder was twice Lord Mayor of Newcastle and also had mercantile interests in London. In 1746, at the age of 32, Matthew the younger inherited the considerable estates 'said to be worth £400,000' of a childless kinsman and family friend, Sir Henry Fetherston, 2nd and last Baronet of Hassingbrook Hall, Essex, who also left generous legacies to Matthew's parents, brothers and sisters. Matthew petitioned for a baronetcy, which was granted him on 3 January 1747. On 24 December 1746 he married Sarah Lethieullier (1722–88), the daughter of Christopher Lethieullier, a director of the Bank of England, and his second wife, Sarah Lascelles.

The English Lethieulliers are descended from Jan le Thieullier, a Huguenot martyred by the Spanish in 1567 or 1568 at Valenciennes, then in Flanders. The martyr's grandson, also Jan, emigrated to England in 1605 and became a prominent City merchant. Sarah, Lady Fetherstonhaugh was his great-granddaughter and was closely related to nearly every influential Huguenot family in England. Seated at Belmont, Middlesex, with a London house in Fenchurch Street, Sarah's branch of the Lethieullier family was rich and cultivated, sharing the artistic interests of their cousin, Smart Lethi-

eullier, FRS, FSA, an antiquary and collector of medals, drawings, sculpture and fossils. Sarah herself painted the two watercolours of flora and fauna in the Red Drawing Room and is said to have brought the famous Uppark doll's-house (see p.83), which bears the Lethieullier arms, into the family. Sarah's half-brothers, Joshua and Lascelles Iremonger, her mother's children by her first husband, were part of her extensive family circle. The Iremongers lived at Wherwell Priory, Hampshire, within easy reach of Uppark. Sir Matthew's own interests, ranging from business to agriculture, from science to the visual arts, from national to local politics, matched those of the Lethieulliers and

(Left) Sir Matthew Fetherstonhaugh; by Pompeo Batoni, 1751 (Little Parlour)

(Right) Sarah Lethieullier, who married Sir Matthew in 1746; by Pompeo Batoni, 1751 (Little Parlour)

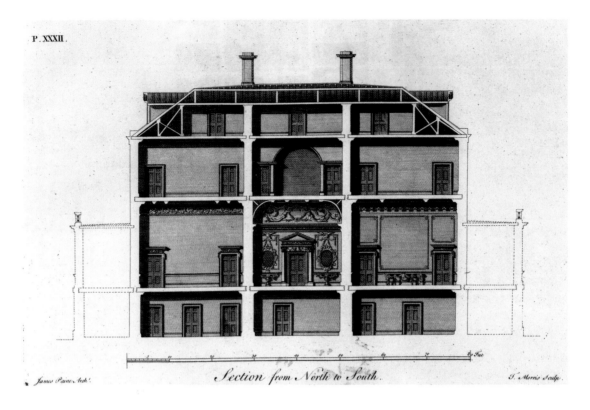

P. XXXII.

James Paine Arch[t].   *Section from North to South.*   T. Morris Sculp.

Sir Matthew's London house in Whitehall, which was built by James Paine, 1754–8; plate xxxii from Paine's 'Plans . . . of Noblemen and Gentlemen's Houses' (1767)

Iremongers. Their friendship and connections are immortalised in the series of portraits by Arthur Devis dated 1748 and 1749, and by Pompeo Batoni, painted in Rome (1751–2).

Sir Matthew embarked upon extensive alterations at Uppark soon after his marriage. This is borne out by his personal Account Book (1747–67), whose terse entries remain almost the sole record of his remodelling, redecoration and refurnishing of Uppark. The book itself was destroyed in the 1989 fire (only fragments remain) and our knowledge of its contents derives from published extracts and from a partial transcription. On 18 February 1747 Sir Matthew recorded the payment of £57 15s 6d 'On acct., of building at Uppark'. Subsequent entries chart the progress of building and furnishing, including payments for slating, glazing, plumbing, locks, chimneypieces, furniture and pictures. After

the entry for 12 November 1749, Sir Matthew observed: 'About this time I went abroad till September 29 1751'. There are no entries in the Account Book during his Grand Tour, although this was a prolific period for acquisitions of pictures and furniture on the Continent. Regular entries resumed again on 1 January 1753. Up to 1 January 1759 Sir Matthew spent £16,615 15s on 'Uppark, beside furniture' – £7,500 being laid out before the Grand Tour and £7,500 between 1751 and 1756. It would seem that work was in abeyance during his absence on the Continent, and the second phase of work at Uppark proceeded concurrently with the erection (1754–8) of his London house.

By contrast to Uppark, Fetherstonhaugh House, Whitehall, is well documented, although most relevant references in Sir Matthew's Account Book between 1754 and 1758 could apply to either. The architect was James Paine, who published a description with engravings in the first volume (1767) of his *Plans, Elevations and Sections of Noblemen and Gentlemen's Houses*. The building, altered by Henry

Holland in 1787, is now the Scottish Office, and stands on the St James's Park side of Whitehall between Horse Guards and Downing Street. There are striking similarities to Uppark, whose interior decoration is also closely comparable to that of other houses by Paine. It is therefore possible to attribute the eighteenth-century work at Uppark to Paine with some degree of certainty.

James Paine's practice had been established in the north of England, but he was also closely associated with the group of London artists and architects within the orbit of the St Martin's Lane Academy, founded by William Hogarth in 1734. The architect Isaac Ware was probably the greatest influence on him. Ware had translated Palladio, and was also a leading member of the Academy, which did much to promote the Rococo style in England. These twin threads, of the English Palladian tradition and the Rococo, run through the eighteenth-century decoration and furnishing of Uppark. Paine took a close interest in the details of his interiors, occasionally designing furniture as well as chimneypieces and plasterwork.

It is unclear exactly when Paine first came to the notice of Sir Matthew, who wrote after 1760, that he had 'been recommended to Mr James Pain of St Martin's Lane architect' for the building of his Whitehall house, begun in 1754. This phrase (in Sir Matthew's handwriting) apparently indicates no prior connection between the two. To counteract this, there is the tantalising entry in Sir Matthew's Account Book on 17 May 1749: 'at Paines 1.3.0'. And on stylistic grounds as well, Paine's hand is detectable at Uppark in the redecoration undertaken for Sir Matthew in the late 1740s and early 1750s. The principal surviving elements of this campaign are the plasterwork ceiling of the Staircase Hall, and in the rooms along the west side of the house – the ceilings in the Red and Little Drawing Rooms and the woodwork in the Tapestry Room.

The argument for Paine's early involvement at Uppark is strengthened by the mention in Sir Matthew's accounts of two craftsmen used by him, not only after 1754, when they would also have been at work in Whitehall, but previously between 1747 and 1749 – Thomas Carter and John Bladwell.

Carter was responsible for the marble chimneypieces in the Saloon and the Stone Hall, which contain plaques superbly carved with classical subjects. In 1764 Edward Gibbon, the historian of the Roman Empire, and Sir Matthew's near-neighbour at Buriton, described Trajan's Column as 'wrought into bas-reliefs with as much taste and delicacy as any chimney piece at Up-park'. John Bladwell, furniture-maker and upholsterer, was paid over £1,000 for supplying general furnishings, which may have included the gilt side-tables in the Saloon and the parcel gilt side-table in the Servery. In addition, the painter-stainer Thomas Bromwich was paid £45 16s in 1748, presumably for wallpaper.

Perhaps the closest comparable house to Uppark in the context of Paine's earlier *oeuvre* is Felbrigg, Norfolk (also National Trust), where the interior was remodelled (1751–6) for William Windham II. The commission probably derived from Windham's friendship with the painter Francis Hayman, another *habitué* of the St Martin's Lane Academy. Windham and Fetherstonhaugh were near-contemporaries, with similar tastes; both had made a collection in Italy, and employed Paine to trans-

The head of Homer from one of the Saloon chimneypieces carved by Thomas Carter c.1750 for Sir Matthew

form an older house for its display. In addition, both commissioned furniture from John Bladwell. Windham had been in touch with Paine soon after his accession to Felbrigg in 1749, the year in which the first phase of work at Uppark presumably came to an end with Sir Matthew's departure for the Continent.

Sir Matthew had travelled abroad before, according to an entry in his Account Book for May 1748: 'Expended abroad . . . £700'. He made purchases at Spa, in Belgium, and Teniers tapestries as well as Dutch and Flemish pictures could have been the spoils of this preliminary tour. Taking the waters at Spa was probably recommended as a cure. Soon after 12 November 1749 he embarked with his wife, Sarah, on a two-year journey that took them to the principal Italian cities. Sir Horace Mann, the British Resident in Florence and correspondent of Horace Walpole, informed Thomas Pelham on 17 October 1750 that he had been invited to dine with them: 'Perhaps you do not know who the Fetherstones are. Sir Matthew is a very sick baronet . . . my lady is sister to Mr Iremonger and Mr Lethieullier who are here and occupying your house. They are all vastly rich.' Sir Matthew remembered in 1767 that 'a constant loss of blood' had reduced him 'so near to dying when I was abroad', and ill-health dogged him throughout his life. Mann's letter also reveals that in 1750 the family group already included Sir Matthew's brother, Utrick (d.1778), and Katherine Durnford, the daughter of the Vicar of Harting. Mann described Miss Durnford as Lady Fetherstonhaugh's 'young companion':

. . . to whom I think Sir Matthew's brother seems very sweet, she was a beauty before the small pox which she had in France robbed her of part of it, which is so much the greater loss as by being the parson of the parish's daughter I suppose it was her chief fortune. She will still be very pretty when the red spots are gone off.

On their return Katherine married Utrick, who was appointed Rector of Harting in 1757. The other members of the party were Sarah's brother, Benjamin Lethieullier (1728/9–97), and half-brother, Lascelles Iremonger (1718/19–93). All the travellers sat to Pompeo Batoni for portraits dated 1751 or 1752.

There were no fewer than nine portraits by Batoni at Uppark until the fire, when one was burnt. Such a long series is unique, though three sitters were painted twice: Sir Matthew, Sarah and Lascelles. In addition, Sir Matthew commissioned two subject pictures from Batoni: female personifications of *Meekness* and *Purity of Heart*, which have hung in the Saloon since at least the early nineteenth century. Sir Matthew liked buying pictures in sets, presumably with an eye for their decorative effect. In Rome, the group also patronised the fashionable French landscape painter Joseph Vernet. Vernet's order book records that it was 'M. Latheulier Anglais' (presumably Benjamin Lethieullier) who commissioned the six pictures now at Uppark, possibly on Lascelles Iremonger's behalf. 'Four must represent marine subjects and the four parts of the day; the two others landscapes with cascades etc.; the price is 100 Roman écus each promised for the end of April 1751.' Perhaps inspired by these magical paintings, Sir Matthew himself ordered two marines and two landscapes in April 1751 and, in March 1752, Benjamin (who stayed on in Rome) ordered a further two landscapes or marines (as the artist chose) on Sir Matthew's behalf. These pictures seem never to have been painted by Vernet, who returned to France in 1753. But Sir Matthew had already acquired instead remarkably faithful copies of the Lethieullier set by Vernet's former assistant, Charles-François Lacroix de Marseille. The Lethieullier Vernets were at Uppark by the early nineteenth century, so Benjamin presumably bequeathed them to his nephew, Sir Harry, in 1797.

In Rome or previously, Sir Matthew and his relations fell in with a group of cultivated Irishmen of similar tastes. Sir Matthew and Lascelles Iremonger were caricatured in Joshua Reynolds's parody (1751; National Gallery of Ireland) of Raphael's *School of Athens*, which was painted for Joseph Henry of Straffan, Co. Kildare. Henry's uncle, Joseph Leeson, later 1st Earl of Milltown, had been in 1744 one of Batoni's first British sitters and was again in Rome in 1750–2, with his son. In 1750 Leeson had received from Vernet four landscapes illustrative of the times of day, a commission that preceded Benjamin Lethieullier's. The pictures still hang in the drawing-room of Leeson's Irish seat,

Joseph Vernet's 'Storm and Shipwreck: Midday', from the 'Four Times of Day' series commissioned in Rome in 1750 and now hanging in the Dining Room

Russborough, Co. Wicklow. Leeson also commissioned two scagliola table-tops from the Florentine monk Don Petro Belloni (see p.54). Again, Leeson's order (1744) preceded Sir Matthew's, though the surviving table-top at Russborough is dated 1750: Don Petro, who lived at the monastery of Vallombrosa, near Florence, was a slow worker. Sir Matthew, who perhaps ordered his pair in 1750, recorded in 1754 a payment of £25 for '2 tables at Florence on acct', which suggests they were still incomplete (one is dated 1754). The white and gold Rococo stands were made in England, probably by Bladwell.

In Venice Sir Matthew acquired eight copies of views of the city by Antonio Canaletto (four

were destroyed in 1989). His Account Book entry (1 January 1753) 'To Mr Smith of Venice £189 9 9' probably refers to this transaction. Consul Joseph Smith was an important patron of contemporary Venetian painters, whose collection (acquired *en bloc* by George III in 1762) was displayed in his Venetian *palazzo* and in his villa on the Brenta. The originals of the Uppark cityscapes were engraved by Andrea Visentini (1735), and Sir Matthew owned a set of these engravings (also destroyed in 1989). Smith, who acted as agent for several Grand Tourists, was paid in 1754 'for Duty on Pictures and China, freight etc £17 15 0'.

Sir Matthew also purchased five views of Naples by Tommaso Ruiz, who supplied similar groups of pictures in 1741 and 1746. Sir Matthew certainly visited Naples and he may also have bought there the set of six large pictures illustrating the Parable of the Prodigal Son by the seventeenth-century

Neapolitan artist Luca Giordano. Other paintings probably acquired in Italy include sets of landscapes by Francesco Zuccarelli (Saloon) and Frans van Bloemen, as well as a pair of still-lives of dead game by Jacob Xavier Vermoelen, one of which is signed and dated 'Roma 1751' (Stone Hall).

Sir Matthew was therefore the purchaser of the majority of the pictures at Uppark; his son, Sir Harry, was to concentrate on the decorative arts. The sets of pictures by the same artist, provided with uniform gilt frames in England, were presumably acquired with an eye to consistency of effect within the rooms at Uppark and in the future house in London. We do not know how the collection was split between the two, but at that time landed collectors tended to concentrate the cream of their pictures in the capital, where they could more readily be seen; family portraits were kept in the country seat. This may explain the curiously dismissive verdict of Horace Walpole on the contents of Uppark on 16 August 1770: 'no tolerable pictures but five or six of Sir Matthew, his Wife, and their relations by Pomeio [sic]

Batoni'. It may suggest, too, that the large Giordanos (which Walpole is unlikely to have ignored) were not yet in the house.

After his return to England on 29 September 1751, Sir Matthew continued the alterations at Uppark, gradually inserting his Grand Tour purchases into newly decorated interiors. The magnificent Rococo pier-glasses (in the Red and Little Drawing Rooms) were commissioned in the early 1750s. The exotic Japanned 'pagoda' cabinet (in the Little Parlour), incorporating Italian ivories and *pietra dura* panels, was probably bought for this room, which was hung with painted Chinese wallpaper. Sir Matthew also embarked upon the construction of the new house in Whitehall, but around 1760 fell out with Paine over his fees. Paine had asked £200 for his services, but Sir Matthew 'would give no more than £150' and though the lower fee was agreed at the time, it later became a bone of contention. In 1760 he sent Sir Matthew a further bill for £557 for work on the London house, a claim which was resisted. The total cost of the building was £10,400.

One of two scagliola table-tops made in Florence by Don Petro Belloni for Sir Matthew (photographed before the fire)

The Saloon ceiling, c.1770, attributed to Paine, which was the climax of Sir Matthew's redecoration of Uppark

The outcome of the dispute is not known, but patron and architect seem to have settled their differences, as Paine was probably responsible around 1770 for the most splendid phase in Sir Matthew's redecoration of Uppark – the Saloon. The ceiling of the old Great Hall was lowered and replastered with a design that combines a coffered central oval in the Palladian style with freer arabesque ornament in the surrounding compartments and coving, and down the walls. In the London house Paine had employed Joseph Rose the Elder, who had not worked in the capital before and was to go on to become one of the greatest decorative plasterers of the age. The Saloon ceiling at Uppark is worthy of him, but unfortunately the craftsman responsible for it is not recorded. Fixed plaster frames were provided for full-length portraits of the King and Queen and for two of the Giordanos,

complemented by richly carved doorcases, to create an ensemble of haunting beauty. The plasterwork ceiling of the Little Parlour also dates from around 1770 and again was probably designed by Paine, but in a more Neo-classical style.

During the 1760s Sir Matthew continued to use craftsmen employed elsewhere by Paine, such as the upholsterer and cabinetmaker John Cobb, mentioned in Sir Matthew's accounts in 1764, and the upholsterer Paul Saunders. Other important craftsmen whose surnames appear in the Account Book include (in 1765) Cobb's partner, William Vile, and Isaac Gosset, who made several wax portraits (destroyed in 1989), and who could also have supplied picture frames.

The location of the London house in Whitehall was convenient for the House of Commons, to which Sir Matthew was elected in 1755, as MP for Morpeth, Northumberland. In 1761 he renounced his northern constituency in favour of nearby Portsmouth, which he represented until his death.

In April 1761 he wrote to the Duke of Newcastle – head of the Whig party, owner of a Sussex estate at Halland, and Prime Minister (1754–6 and 1757–62) – thanking him for having:

recommended me to so worthy a set of gentlemen as this corporation seems to consist of; for everything was done with great order and decency; and after the election was over we finished the evening with great mirth and jollity.

Sir Matthew never spoke in the Commons, but remained Newcastle's staunch political ally and became a close friend.

Sir Matthew also pursued his business interests. He was among the biggest holders of Bank of England and East India stock. His late father-in-law was a director of the Bank, his brother-in-law a director and Deputy Governor. His East India holdings (averaging £16,000) gave him considerable voting strength: he supported Clive of India at a time of expanding British interests in the subcontinent. References to merchant ships and Indiamen in which he had invested appear in his Account Book from March 1747. He was a promoter of the colonisation of America (see p.88); he also owned a lead-mine and presumably inherited his father's coal-mines in 1762. In 1746–7 he sold £42,000 worth of stock, perhaps with a view to buying and altering Uppark. As well as playing the stock market, he was an *habitué* of the gaming table. White's, the St James's Coffee House and Almack's are mentioned in the Account Book. From time to time, he summarised his position: in 1758 a lengthy calculation showed the 'Balance in Favour' between 1748 and 1760 as £418 10s 6d. In 1758 he won £1,007 8s. In more sober mood, he speculated as to the relative costs of living in town or in the country. He enjoyed both, observing in 1768: 'No-one experiences more than myself the difference between a busy London life and the tranquil rural Scenes of the Country. Each have their amusements; and I believe give a zest to each other.'

A cultivated and erudite man in possession of a good library, Sir Matthew's scientific interests earned him election as a Fellow of the Royal Society in 1752. The Society's records describe him as 'a Gentleman of Literature and Improvement and versed in Natural Knowledge'. He has been credited with the authorship of a manuscript on *Natural Philosophy*, including observations on electricity, which survived until 1989 among the papers. He owned an 'Air Pump', a microscope and a telescope.

Sir Matthew's Account Book also records charitable donations: 'Gave a Poor Man £1.1.0.', and gifts to hospitals where he was a governor (one of which, the Middlesex, was rebuilt by James Paine, 1755–78). However, gaiety was never far away; he subscribed to the Opera, the Jockey Club and spent money at Ascot races, at Ranelagh Gardens and on clothes: 'for Satin for a Waistcoat £3.1.0.'. The Account Book also cryptically charts the progress of Sir Matthew and Sarah's only child, Henry (always called Harry), who was born at Uppark on 22 December 1754. On 1 March 1758 'Harry's Buttins' was followed by 'Harry toys'. Another 1758 entry – Reynolds £25.4.0.' – may refer to a part-payment for the full-length portrait (destroyed 1989) which depicted Harry at about this date. Sir Matthew had his son inoculated against smallpox the following year, when this was still fairly novel. The accounts continue: 'Mapps for Harry' (1760), 'Writing Master for Harry', 'Harry's Masters', 'Harry's Horse', 'Harry's Purse and Gloves', 'Cutting Harry's hair', 'Watch for Harry' (all 1761). In 1763 Sir Matthew informed the Duke of Newcastle that Harry was an 'amusing Companion' and that he hoped 'one day to receive great Comfort from so sweet a Disposition as he seems blessed with'. In 1764 Newcastle heard that his 'Young Friend . . . must be kept to his book: he has but too much pleasure, tho' he is a very good boy'. Harry's education was entrusted to Dr Durnford, the Vicar of Harting, until he went to Eton in 1767. There Harry remained until 1771 and he went up to University College, Oxford in 1772.

Harry appears to have enjoyed good health, whereas his father's recurrent illnesses seem to have prejudiced his political advancement. By 1768 Sir Matthew, who suffered from gout, had decided that 'Nature, temperance and good Kitchen Physick' were preferable to medical remedies. However, on 2 December 1772 the Duke of Richmond informed Edmund Burke that Sir Matthew 'had been in a very dangerous illness for several months. He is now better . . . but fears, and with great reasons, that if he was to venture out . . . it might cost him his life.' Edward Gibbon noted that Sir Matthew 'was breaking up very fast'. He died two years later on 18 March 1774 'at his house in Whitehall'.

Soon after Sir Matthew's death, Gibbon observed: 'At present everything carries the appearance of sobriety and economy. The Baronet, instead of flying to Paris and Rome, returns to his College at Oxford, and even the house in Whitehall is to be let.' However, Sir Harry's natural exuberance and extravagance were clearly evident by 31 January 1775, when Gibbon wrote perceptively: 'Sir Harry is very civil and good-humoured. But from the unavoidable temper of youth, I fear he will cost many a tear to Lady F.' He added that she 'consults everybody, but has neither authority nor plan'.

Sir Matthew owed £18,602, which was paid off by raising £37,255 through the sale of property, investments and timber. His will (19 March 1774) stipulated that his widow should receive £3,000 and an extra £200 per annum. Sarah and her brother Benjamin Lethieullier were entrusted with the care of Harry until he was 21 (in 1775). Harry was the sole residuary legatee, after bequests to Sir Matthew's brothers and relations, and of a year's salary to the 28 indoor and fifteen outdoor servants who, in Sir Matthew's lifetime, moved between Uppark and Whitehall.

After coming down from Oxford, Sir Harry made the Grand Tour of Europe with his uncle, the Rev. Utrick Fetherstonhaugh, who had been of the party in 1749–51. They visited Paris, Geneva,

Prophet and Surprise, racehorses owned by Sir Matthew; by John Boultbee (Staircase Hall)

Venice, Florence, Rome and Naples. In 1776 Sir Harry followed the family tradition of sitting to Pompeo Batoni, whose fame (and charges) had increased considerably since 1751. (The portrait now hangs over the fireplace in the Red Drawing Room.) In 1812 he remembered that 'I never suffered so much cold as I did in the winter I passed in Italy'. Apart from the Batoni portrait, there is no record of acquisitions on the tour, which left Sir Harry with a lasting appreciation of French culture in particular.

On Sir Harry's return, his mother managed his household, but in 1778 she discovered that he had run through £3,324 in a few months. Perhaps as a result, the family's ancestral seat in Northumberland was sold the following year. He wrote of 'shivering in the old Gothic hall of Featherstone Castle with only a frigid sense of its antiquity'. The London house in Whitehall was also disposed of in 1787 for 12,000 guineas. In 1780 he began his celebrated liaison with Emma Hart, the future wife of the cultivated British ambassador at Naples, Sir William Hamilton, and lover of Lord Nelson. Sir Harry is said to have discovered her in a London establishment, euphemistically named 'The Temple of Health', which promised to prolong 'Human Life, Healthily and Happily to the very longest Period of Human Existence'. Emma lived on the Uppark estate until November 1781, when she was packed off to Cheshire six months pregnant. The following January she wrote to Charles Greville:

Believe me I am allmost distraktid. I have never hard from Sir H. and he is not at Lechster [Leicester] now, I am sure, what shall I dow, good God what shall I dow, I have wrote 7 letters and no anser, I cant come to town for want of mony, I have not a farthing to bless myself with and I think my frends looks cooly on me.

Thirty years later, when she had again fallen on hard times, Sir Harry took pity on her: 'No one better deserves to be happy.' He sent money and game from the Uppark larder, and invited her down for 'a view of old Uppark dans la belle saison'.

The tradition that Emma danced naked on the Dining Room table suggests that she had been the principal ornament of a somewhat raffish circle, which must have met when Sir Harry's mother was

safely absent. During the Prince of Wales's visits in 1784 and 1785, Lady Fetherstonhaugh stayed with her Iremonger relations at Wherwell. Her niece, Elizabeth Iremonger, wrote in 1785 that she and her aunt had vacated their places at Uppark 'to the Prince and his Party. The entertainment was to last three days; great preparations were making to render it completely elegant; Races of all sorts were to be upon the most beautiful Spot of Ground I believe that England can produce.' Often riding his own horses, Sir Harry competed for prize money and for the silver-gilt trophy inscribed 'The Prince's Cup Uppark 1785' (now in the Dining Room). According to Mrs Montagu, there were 'various other divertimenti fit for children of six foot high'. The Prince 'was much delighted and said that Newmarket Races were dull in comparison'. Betting, gambling and good living were essential ingredients of these summer parties, whose exquisite cuisine was provided by Sir Harry's French chef, Moget. In 1799 a prospective visitor to Uppark was informed : 'Sir Henry himself can have no attraction but his cook and his money, for he is, I believe, the greatest goose that ever existed.'

Sir Harry also advised the Prince on the acquisition of works of art and their display, being one of a group of advisers that included Lord Yarmouth, later 3rd Marquess of Hertford, and Sir Thomas Lawrence. The French furniture, porcelain and fittings Sir Harry bought for Uppark reflect his and the Prince's predominantly francophile tastes. Unfortunately, several of the finest pieces, including furniture by Riesener and Carlin, were sold in 1910. The 1910 valuation for sale also shows that Sir Harry collected elaborate sixteenth-century German silver, an antiquarian taste shared by the Prince, but perhaps most closely associated with William Beckford.

Sir Harry visited France in 1802–3, during the Peace of Amiens, in 1819 and in 1824. A few receipts record purchases in Paris, which included furniture, clocks, silk and Sèvres porcelain, and in 1819 he was considering the acquisition of a Parisian

(Right) Sir Harry Fetherstonhaugh, who was also painted by Batoni on the Grand Tour, in 1776 (Red Drawing Room)

hôtel. From at least 1810 he was acquainted with Humphry Repton, the architect and landscape designer. Their friendship may have derived from Repton's connections with the Prince of Wales. In 1813 he produced garden designs for the Prince's London palace, Carlton House, and in 1808 published proposals, inspired by Indian architecture, for the rebuilding of the Brighton Pavilion. Repton's hopes 'ended in nothing', the Pavilion commission being given to his rival, John Nash. 'Cursed is the man who puts his trust in princes', concluded Repton in a letter to Sir Harry in 1814.

Sir Harry had also become estranged from the Prince. All was well in 1803, when a royal visit to Uppark was the prelude to a naval review. By 1810 friends at Court were rebutting 'prejudiced and poisoned' vituperation against Sir Harry. In 1811 he was upset by his exclusion from a fête at Carlton House. He had increasingly to find consolation in a country life, and even considered writing his memoirs. None the less, his winter shooting parties continued in great style, and the tradition

that he became a recluse appears to be exaggerated.

His exile from royal circles and his friendship with Repton encouraged Sir Harry to make alterations to Uppark, probably for the first time. Repton's Red Book, dated August 1810, set out the initial proposals, which included the linking of the main house to the service pavilions by colonnades. The works as executed were less grandiose. The main entrance was moved from the east to the north, where the Portland stone portico was constructed in 1812–13. A stone-coloured passage, top-lit by stained-glass windows, led via an elaborately nailed crimson baize door to the Staircase Hall. The Dining Room was panelled in seventeenth-century style (Repton and Sir Harry both thought the house had been built by Inigo Jones). With a Servery lit by a huge stained-glass window, it was conceived as a monument to Sir Harry's political allegiances, incorporating busts of Whig worthies and of Napoleon. Repton also supplied around 1815 the pair of bookcases on the north wall of the Saloon and repainted the room white and

Repton's proposal for Uppark from his Red Book of 1810

gold (the same décor he had used in the new Dining Room).

After Repton's alterations, which were complete by *c*.1815, the accounts are silent about Sir Harry's treatment of the house until 1826. From then until 1841 the bills presented by a London painter, Charles B. Pepper, indicate regular interior and exterior redecoration. In the Saloon, however, only the window embrasures were repainted and gilded, the remainder being 'repaired' or preserved by 'Scowering and Cleaning'. Pepper was also commissioned to paint the servants' quarters and outbuildings. In fact, very few local tradesmen were employed by either Sir Matthew or Sir Harry and even the meat and fish were sent down from London.

Repton died in 1818, and his place as friend and architectural adviser was taken by Charles Heathcote Tatham, a scholarly Neo-classical architect, who published several influential books illustrated by engravings after the Antique or his own designs. Again, the connection was probably due to the Prince of Wales. Tatham's master, Henry Holland, was primarily responsible for Carlton House, for which his brother, Thomas Tatham, supplied furniture. Unexecuted designs by C. H. Tatham for a Neo-classical temple (1822), a Gothick lodge (1823) and for alterations to Uppark itself existed in the house archives. He and his brother's firm may also have been responsible for supplying a set of ivory inlaid ebony furniture which was also destroyed in the 1989 fire.

After Waterloo a palatial seat was sought for the victorious Duke of Wellington. In 1816 the Uppark estate was suggested as a potential site for a new building, but Sir Harry could think of nowhere suitable 'unless I make over Uppark to the Duke and retire to a warm Climate, as every old Batchelor should at my time of life'. A correspondence ensued between the Duke and Sir Harry which was quickly terminated when the price of Uppark was fixed at £90,000. If Sir Harry was reluctant to sell, the Duke, it is said, was also put off by the steepness of the hill from Harting village. 'I have crossed the Alps once,' he declared.

On 12 September 1825, in the Saloon at Uppark, Sir Harry married Mary Ann Bullock (1805–74),

his 20-year-old dairymaid. He was over 70, and apparently declared to his gamekeeper: 'I've made a fool of myself, Legge.' 'I hear Sir Harry Fetherston is to marry his cook,' wrote Mrs Arbuthnot to the Duke of Wellington. Mary Ann was reputedly sent to Paris to acquire the social graces, and despite the initial sensation, the marriage lasted.

In 1830 Edward Bailey furnished 'her Ladyship's Dressing Room' with blue satin upholstery and festoon curtains, with the pictures hung from 'handsome silk bows and rosettes' on 'very strong and gold coloured twisted silk Rope'. Several Brussels and Saxony carpets were supplied by Watson, Wood & Bell, Old Bond Street, between 1835 and 1840, including a bordered carpet 'in rich colours' for the main staircase. In 1832 the Dairy, where his wife had once presided, was embellished by Sir Harry with the existing stained glass and white tiles with a 'Rich Enamelled Flower Border'.

The census return provides a vignette of the occupants of Uppark in 1841. Lady Fetherstonhaugh's younger sister, Frances Bullock (1818–95), had joined the ménage soon after 1825 and had been educated by Sir Harry's protégée, Ann Sutherland (1804–93). William Garthorne (aged 71) was described as an 'Architect' (he had supervised Repton's alterations) and there were 10 male and 13 female servants. Joseph Weaver (aged 30) was Sir Harry's valet, like his father before him, and both were taxidermists and conchologists whose arrangements of stuffed birds and shells were once a feature of the house. Joseph Weaver the Younger contributed thirteen chapters on flora and fauna to the Rev. H. D. Gordon's *History of Harting*, published in 1877.

In June 1838 Sir Harry was supplied by Edward Bailey with 'a large handsome mahogany invalid chair . . . covered with green Utrecht velvet'. Mary Ann had to act as his amanuensis on more than one occasion when he was 'plagued with the Gout in his right hand'. Her letter-book reveals that she and her husband led an increasingly sheltered life. Sir Harry died on 24 October 1846, at the age of 90.

CHAPTER FOUR

MARY ANN AND FRANCES FETHERSTONHAUGH

The period between Sir Harry's death in 1846 and the death of his sister-in-law in 1895 has been described as a 'long Victorian afternoon'. According to the traditional version of events, Lady Fetherstonhaugh (who died in 1874) and her sister were devoted to the preservation of Uppark 'as Sir 'Arry 'ad it'. Thus Uppark 'survived untouched, a sleeping beauty house' unscathed by regrettable Victorian alterations. This was true up to a point. Even after the 1989 fire, the Saloon and Dining Room retain much of the paint and gilding applied by Repton. Shadows on the wall still indicate how Sir Harry arranged the pictures, which are hung in the same places. The impression of time stood still was fostered by Uppark's conservative and enlightened twentieth-century owners. Lady Meade-Fetherstonhaugh's rejuvenation of the textiles and wallpapers in the 1930s was the principal element of Uppark's fame as a miraculous eighteenth-century survival.

The reality was rather different. Sir Harry himself died in the ninth year of Victoria's reign. His widow continued to patronise London tradesmen, including painters, furniture-makers, carpet manufacturers and upholsterers. In 1851 and 1859 Henry Piper of Eastcheap and Thomas Harland of Southwark supplied red, crimson and satin flock wallpapers. The 'drawing room' hung in 1859 could have been either the Red or Little Drawing Room. 'Satin flock' describes the paper of about this date in the Little Drawing Room, which still retains the 'mauve and crimson figured stripe Merino damask' curtains provided by Charles Hindley of Oxford Street in 1852. The fire revealed that the faded red flock of the Red Drawing Room had an earlier and probably eighteenth-century red flock beneath, so the later flock (partially restored to the room) could well have been put up in the 1850s. The elaborate French and English wallpapers upstairs (still *in situ*

before the fire and recently copied) must also have been due to Lady Fetherstonhaugh. In 1859 she commissioned repainting that affected all the principal rooms to a greater or lesser degree. Again, in May 1862, 166 yards (presumably of panelling) was painted 'twice oil and flatted in white', and several ceilings and cornices were redecorated. In 1853 the Servants' Hall and Housekeeper's Room were redecorated by a Chichester painter, R. Randall. In 1865 many of the sash-windows were reglazed with large panes of 'British Plate'. In 1860 the 'Hot Water Boiler for Warming the House' (presumably part of the system installed by Sir Harry in 1835) was replaced, as was the kitchen range and downstairs pipework.

The 1851 census shows that 'Dame Mary Anne Fetherstonhaugh' was the owner of 5,149 acres, employing 203 labourers. The house staff included a butler, two footmen, a housekeeper (Mary Finegan), a cook (Esther Chesterfield), at least four housemaids and a laundress. Sarah Neal, the daughter of a Chichester innkeeper, was lady's maid to Frances Bullock, Lady Fetherstonhaugh's sister. Her first impressions (in 1850) were of 'very quaint odd people' living in a large house with 'pretty tapestry and a pretty park with deer'. Sarah, who had been trained in dressmaking, millinery and hairdressing, became 'greatly attached' to her employer. She had reluctantly to resign her post in 1853, having married Joseph Wells, an Uppark gardener turned Bromley shopkeeper and professional cricketer. Their youngest son, Bertie, was the writer H. G. Wells, whose autobiography contains an important memoir of Uppark. The house also appears, thinly disguised as 'Bladesover', in his novel *Tono-Bungay* (1909).

(Right) Mary Ann Bullock, the Uppark dairymaid who married Sir Harry in 1825

Lady Fetherstonhaugh and her sister, Frances (who took the name and arms of Fetherstonhaugh on inheriting Uppark in 1874) perpetuated Sir Harry's tradition of hospitality. There were winter shooting parties and the house was lent to friends for their honeymoons: the 2nd Lord and Lady Leconfield (of Petworth) in 1867 and the 5th Earl and Countess Winterton (of Shillinglee Park, near Petworth) in 1882. Lady Leconfield recalled that 'at Harting Station we were met by a hired carriage and pair with a postillion. On going up Harting Hill, he got off, and could not get on again, so that Henry had to get out to assist him. He apologised to me afterwards for having said damn in my presence.'

Lady Fetherstonhaugh was famous locally for her good works, which are commemorated in a stained-glass window, installed by Joseph Weaver in South Harting church, where Sir Harry's tomb (1846) is by Richard Westmacott the Younger. Lady Fetherstonhaugh donated an extension to the churchyard in memory of her friendship with Ann Sutherland, who carved the base of the church font. The comprehensive inventory of Uppark taken after her

Frances Bullock, who inherited Uppark on the death of her sister Mary Ann in 1874 and took the name Fetherstonhaugh

death in 1874 (by the Petworth firm Death & Son) is the first to have survived since that of 1722.

Miss Fetherstonhaugh and Miss Sutherland's regime was still remembered when Lady Meade-Fetherstonhaugh came to Uppark in 1931. She recorded that:

[the old ladies] always dressed in velvet as they thought it suited the house best. The footmen wore long button-holes of freshly cut hothouse flowers every day with stalks the length of daffodils and Miss F. had said 'I cannot understand why people make such a fuss what to call their footmen. I call one "'Enery" and the other "Hedward".'

In 1880 Mrs Wells, who had resigned as lady's maid in 1853, returned to Uppark as housekeeper. According to H. G. Wells:

She knew at least how a housekeeper should look, and assumed a lace cap, lace apron, black silk dress and all the rest of it, and she knew how a housekeeper should drive down to the tradespeople in Petersfield and take a glass of sherry when the account was settled. She marched down to Church every Sunday morning; the whole downstairs household streamed down the Warren and Harting Hill to Church.

Wells thought his mother 'was perhaps the worst housekeeper that ever was thought of':

It dawned slowly upon Miss Fetherstonhaugh . . . it was manifest from the first to the very competent if totally illiterate, head housemaid Old Ann, who gave herself her own orders more and more. The kitchen, the laundry, the pantry, with varying kindliness, apprehended this inefficiency in the housekeeper's room.

Mrs Wells's diaries reveal her own frustration: '6 Dec [1892] Today Duke of Connaught arrived. Oh! such a fuss and work, how I wish I was out of it.' Miss Fetherstonhaugh and Mrs Wells were increasingly 'two deaf old women at cross-purposes'. 'The rather sentimental affection between them evaporated' and Mrs Wells was dismissed in 1892.

H. G. Wells also wrote of the 'two elderly ladies in the parlour following their shrunken routines'. Here, 'they spent whole days . . . between reading and slumber and caressing their two pet dogs'. Miss Sutherland died in 1893 and Miss Fetherstonhaugh in 1895. Towards the end of Miss Fetherstonhaugh's

Sarah Wells, the mother of the writer H. G. Wells, and the Uppark housekeeper from 1880 to 1892

life, there was considerable speculation as to her heir. She failed to find a suitable blood relation of Sir Harry, despite considerable research. At lunch one day Lady Leconfield was asked what she would do with the silver, should she be given Uppark: 'Take it to Petworth, of course' was the answer. Miss Fetherstonhaugh finally settled upon Lt Col the Hon. Keith Turnour (1848–1930), the younger son of her friends, the 4th Earl and Countess Winterton. As Colonel Turnour's son was already dead, her will specified that he should be succeeded at Uppark by the younger son of the 4th Earl and Countess of Clanwilliam, who were renting nearby Stansted Park.

CHAPTER FIVE

THE TWENTIETH CENTURY

Col. Keith Turnour-Fetherstonhaugh's tenure of Uppark is enshrined in the photographs taken for *Country Life* in 1910. Absent are the French furniture and other artefacts sold in 1910 and said to have been lost with the *Titanic en route* for the Metropolitan Museum in New York. However, the pictures were still hung in the positions recorded in a set of early nineteenth-century diagrams, and so they remained until the 1970s. Indeed, both the Turnour-Fetherstonhaughs and their successors, the Meade-Fetherstonhaughs, were admirably conservative in their care of Uppark. One of Col. Turnour-Fetherstonhaugh's 'few and sensible innovations was to abandon the old kitchen quarters and the elaborate

tunnels by which meals were brought to the house, and to make new dispositions in the basement of the house itself'.

On his death in 1930, Miss Fetherstonhaugh's will stipulated that Uppark should be inherited by Admiral the Hon. Sir Herbert Meade GCVO, CB, DSO (1875–1964). After distinguished service in destroyers during the First World War, Sir Herbert (known as Jim) spent the final stage of his career (until 1936) as Admiral Commanding Royal Yachts. His obituarist called him 'that splendid mixture of sailor and courtier epitomised by Marryat in the term "sea gentleman".' In 1911 he married Margaret Glyn (1888–1977), grand-

Margaret, Lady Meade-Fetherstonhaugh and her daughter Jean showing two Uppark curtains before (right) and after their conservation work, c.1935

Miss Frances Fetherstonhaugh (centre) and her heir
Col. Keith Turnour-Fetherstonhaugh (right) sitting on the
south steps, c.1890–5

daughter of the 8th Duke of Argyll. She was taken, she wrote, 'to stay at Uppark soon after we were married. The marked kindness of our reception was the foundation of many happy visits to Colonel Keith Turnour-Fetherstonhaugh and his daughter.' The house made an indelible impression, and after living in 'twenty houses in twenty years', they returned on 11 February 1931 'to enter into the fairy story of our lives at Uppark'. The 11th Duke of Argyll described her in 1977 'as the visionary behind . . . the complete reinstatement of the building to its former glory' and stated that the Meade-Fetherstonhaughs 'dedicated their lives at very great personal sacrifice to bringing back its furnishings and fabrics to their original 18th-century condition for the world to enjoy after them'.

Lady Meade-Fetherstonhaugh's diaries chronicle the zest and excitement with which the new owners took up their task. The roof was repaired, the structure consolidated and the house was adapted for the requirements of a family with four children. In 1932, by the terms of Miss Fetherstonhaugh's will, the Admiral took the additional surname of Fetherstonhaugh and became, as his crew affectionately called him, 'that bloke with the long-winded name'. Meanwhile Lady Meade-Fetherstonhaugh had found her vocation in the preservation of Uppark's interiors. 'Haven't you thrown those curtains away yet?' exclaimed the friends who 'poured down' to see Uppark. Instead, with the determination of someone for whom 'failure simply did not exist', she embarked upon a pioneering eight years of textile conservation which left curtains, previously in tatters, strong enough to be torn down in one piece by the 1989 firemen. Her diaries and letters reveal the speed with which the techniques were developed. With the advice and help of Mrs Antrobus of the Royal School of Needlework, fragile and filthy window and bed curtains were cleaned 'by being pulled over dewy grass' or by immersion in water infused with the herb *Saponaria officinalis*. The fluffy silk was then laid down by couching thread sewn in parallel lines. These silken 'tramlines', inserted by Lady Meade-Fetherston-haugh and her atelier can still be clearly discerned today. The hangings of the Prince Regent's bed, repaired between 20 May 1931 and 12 November 1932, received in some places 20 rows of stitching to the inch. This close stitching had the desired effect of keeping all the frayed material flat. *Saponaria* was also used for the cleaning of oil paintings, but it was not a panacea, as Lady Meade-Fetherstonhaugh observed in January 1932: 'N.B. I noticed Saponaria is not good for gilt – water gilt.'

Between 1931 and 1934 furniture was fumigated and repaired, china washed, the chandeliers secured and the collection of deeds, manuscripts and papers aired and sorted. Sir Matthew's Account Book emerged from an attic: 'It is horrifying to find such a valuable thing in such a place.' From Lady Meade-Fetherstonhaugh's interest in the family papers came the evocative history of the house, *Uppark and its People* (1964), which she wrote with Oliver Warner. Family, friends and servants were pressed into service. Pascal, the French chef, 'provided a cauldron' for the first experiment with *Saponaria*. The butler, Osborne, helped take down, wash and rehang curtains. He also dismantled and cleaned the chandeliers, which were rehung after repair by the 'Seaman Rigger' of the Royal Yacht *Victoria and Albert*: the replacement suspension cords were 'patent 109 towing line which had been covered by crimson thread in London'. By 1939 Lady Meade-Fetherstonhaugh reckoned that 'we had mended and re-hung twenty-eight brocade curtains, three Queen Anne four-poster beds, and a set of chairs'. After the war, her skills were employed on 'textiles which have been sent to Uppark for repair from Europe and America as well as in Britain'. Lady Meade-Fetherstonhaugh undertook the large-scale conservation of eighteenth-century silk damask at The Vyne in Hampshire, Syon House in Middlesex, and other houses. Her fame grew, and in her eighties she conducted a 'hectic six week lecture tour' of America.

'In 1945, the war over and the future uncertain,' Martin Drury wrote in his preface to the 1988 reprint of *Uppark and its People*:

Admiral Meade-Fetherstonhaugh and his son, Richard, approached the National Trust with an offer of Uppark and land to protect its setting. The Trust's files covering the next nine years are very fat, evidence of the determination of both parties to find a means of endowing the Admiral's gift and the complexity of the resulting negotiations. But Uppark's guardian angel was still at his post. An endowment was put together comprising grants from the Pilgrim and Dulverton Trusts, the gift of some standing timber on the estate from the Admiral and a substantial sum from an anonymous lady who had never seen the house, but whose generosity was stimulated by a description given over the telephone by a member of the Trust's staff. And so, in 1954, Uppark passed to the National Trust.

After her son Richard's death in 1958, and her husband's in 1964, Lady Meàde-Fetherstonhaugh lived at Uppark until 1965 before relinquishing her tenancy to her widowed daughter-in-law and her family. The Meade-Fetherstonhaughs continued to live at Uppark, and the National Trust maintained the family's established policy of preserving Uppark with as little tangible change as possible. Just as Lady Meade-Fetherstonhaugh had avoided redecoration by carefully touching up old paint, so the Trust (with the advice of John Fowler) generally limited its attentions to repainting and regilding shutters and window embrasures which had been bleached by the sunlight. In the 1970s the Little Parlour and Entrance Corridor were redecorated, following complaints (that now seem misguided) about the tattiness of the house. And so Uppark remained a famous and much-loved relic of the past, until 30 August 1989.

(Right) Admiral and Lady Meade-Fetherstonhaugh photographed in the Saloon with their younger son, John, later 7th Earl of Clanwilliam, for the Coronation of 1953

CHAPTER SIX

THE FIRE AND RESCUE OF UPPARK

On 30 August 1989, a hot and breezy day, Uppark had been shrouded in scaffolding for more than a year so that structural and roof repairs could be carried out. This was the last day and workmen were finishing off the leadwork by the pediment on the south front. During their tea break they noticed smoke, but were unable to contain what quickly became a blaze. The fire-alarms had sounded at 3.36pm. The first fire engine arrived from Petersfield a quarter of an hour later. More help was summoned. Within another half-hour there were four engines and another sixteen on their way. At the height of the fire, there were 27 fire-engines and 156 firemen from three county brigades. In the desperate search for water, fire hoses were laid as far as Harting village. The operation was directed by Kenneth Lloyd, Deputy Chief Fire Officer for Sussex, who soon realised that the fire would consume Uppark and concentrated his attention on buying time for the rescue of the contents. Their retrieval is a testimony to the skill and determination of the firemen, who were assisted in the initial stages by National Trust staff, volunteers and members of the Meade-Fetherstonhaugh family. However, the greatest loss was the family's own collection of pictures, furniture and textiles, the contents of an incomparable series of first-floor rooms. Such was the speed of the fire that the upper floors had to be abandoned at an early stage.

By about 5 o'clock the first floor was engulfed by flames, which spread through the collapsed ceilings and within the cavity walls. Downstairs, furniture, pictures and works of art were piled up on the grass. A human chain evacuated the porcelain from the basement. As quickly as possible, rescued objects were removed to temporary storage. Inside, salvage was becoming increasingly hazardous. In the burning Staircase Hall the firemen were drenched by water as they prised Tillemans's large early eight-

eenth-century Uppark landscapes out of the panelling. Soon afterwards, the staircase collapsed. For the next hour, until about six, salvage teams wearing breathing apparatus made rapid sorties into the principal rooms, rescuing what they could.

At 5.15pm newsmen in a helicopter filmed the huge plume of smoke swirling eastwards across the Downs. The camera focused on the ant-like figures rushing hither and thither fighting the flames or rescuing furniture from the Saloon. These were the pictures which appeared on that evening's news. Meanwhile, National Trust switchboards at the Regional Office at Polesden Lacey and in London were jammed with enquiries, thus hampering emergency calls. Specialist conservators, both within and without the Trust, were summoned to Uppark, and essential supplies delivered: polythene sheets, bubble wrap, tissue paper and a host of other materials.

By 6.30 senior National Trust staff had arrived at Uppark. Their relief that so much had been saved from the ground floor was tempered by the realisation that the heavier and fixed furniture, such as pier-tables and glasses were still inside, together with the curtains, pelmets and other fixtures. It was clear that the fire would soon break into these apparently empty rooms, so rapid action was required. The brigade salvage team then began its final phase of work. Damask curtains, given a new lease of life by Lady Meade-Fetherstonhaugh in the 1930s, were pulled down in one piece and wallpaper from the Red Drawing Room was torn off in huge strips. By this time, however, it was unsafe to enter some rooms and it was frustrating to see their contents gradually consumed by fire. The frames of the scagliola tables in the Stone Hall were ignited soon after 6.30pm, whereas the Little Parlour next door remained intact until about 5am, its chandelier swinging in the heat, until a falling chimneystack

Uppark on fire

carried the whole room into the basement. A major triumph at about 9.30pm was the rescue of the three great Rococo pier-glasses in the Red and Small Drawing Rooms, one of them in flames as it was passed sideways through the window. In the course of the night, firemen continued the retrieval but it became increasingly sporadic as the fire progressed.

Dawn revealed the full extent of the damage. An aerial photograph, published in several newspapers, encouraged the erroneous conclusion that Uppark had been 'gutted' by the fire. In fact, the walls still stood (and subsequently required remarkably little structural repair). Although the ceilings had collapsed, and the upper floors were almost completely destroyed, the principal ground-floor rooms retained much of their mural decoration and the marble chimneypieces were still in place. The rooms were filled with heaps of rubble and charred timbers. In the Saloon the ormolu chandelier jutted out of the detritus, indicating the possibility of other survivals within the debris. Miraculously, the Prince Regent's Bed was still intact, and conservators were able to direct the firemen as it was dismantled and passed out through the windows of the Tapestry Room, shortly before the ceiling collapsed.

Picture conservators had been working all night to consolidate paintings that had suffered intense heat and water damage. A second shift relieved them at 8am. By that evening, the paintings left Uppark for storage and eventual treatment elsewhere. For reasons of security as well as conservation, the furniture and other contents that could safely be moved were transported within a further two days. The publicity generated by the fire had increased the risk of theft, but fortunately these precautions prevented it.

The day after the fire inaugurated many weeks of determined action to preserve what could be preserved of the fabric and contents of Uppark. The walls were still standing but they needed buttressing. Scaffolding could not be introduced without clearing the smouldering slag heaps that filled the

The fire destroyed roofs and ceilings, but the walls and much of the decorative woodwork and plasterwork survived

carcass of the building. After most fires, even in important buildings, the debris is simply carted away and dumped. By contrast, after the fire at Hampton Court in 1986, investigation, recording and preservation of what was ostensibly rubbish had brought considerable dividends. Once the fire brigade had officially pronounced that the Uppark fire was out (after four and a half days of damping down), and with watchers strategically placed to warn of any movement of the structure, digging began. Each room (the sequence dictated by the condition of the surrounding walls) was separated into grid squares for the purpose of recording the location of what was removed. In sifting through the wet sludge, interesting fragments were separated and placed in plastic trays labelled with grid

references. Thus it was possible later to determine, for example, that fragments of glass found in the Staircase Hall belonged to the Gothick lantern previously hanging there. This made it possible to replace the glass to the precise dimensions. Given the speed with which this initial sorting had to be carried out, the residue (to be sifted later) was shovelled into dustbins (also marked with grid references). The 3,860 labelled dustbins became a potent symbol of the scale of the salvage operation. This exercise had to be juggled in the first few weeks with the urgent need to shore up the walls.

Discoveries within the house (including the Red Drawing Room Axminster carpet three days after the fire) increased the pressure on conservators already battling to save a huge volume of material. The Trust's Conservation Advisers, supported by large teams, had to adapt to what were dubbed 'field conditions'. The decision to interleave the sodden, filthy and charred curtains in polythene (to keep them wet) followed by gradual drying in large and airy marquees succeeded in avoiding permanent staining. Fragments of decorated plasterwork, ranging from the size of a paperweight to that of a dining-room table, had to be carefully cleaned and consolidated. The larger pieces were faced with paper to inhibit delamination. Stores were filled with remnants of every description, from chimney-pots to picture hooks, which were gradually sorted into categories. It soon became possible to see how much plaster had been saved from the Saloon; how many lengths of gilt-wood fillet had emerged from the Red Drawing Room and so on. A computer system was installed to classify the huge number of fragments (over 12,000 in all), developed from that used after the Hampton Court fire.

Meanwhile, speculation mounted as to the fate of Uppark. A local MP advocated demolition for the benefit of the landscape, arguing that Lord Tankerville would not have received planning permission today. Other pundits argued for either an authentic reconstruction or rebuilding in a modern idiom, or a mixture of the two. To those working on the site it was becoming increasingly evident that enough survived to justify the repair of Uppark, thereby re-creating the setting for an otherwise homeless collection. In addition, the Trust's insurance was designed to cover reinstatement. The decision to restore Uppark to its appearance the day before the fire, 'in so far as that is practicable', was taken on 5 October 1989, less than two months after the fire.

Following the appointment of a 'Design Team' led by the Conservation Practice as architect, it was decided to opt for a management contract which would allow design decisions to be taken gradually as building progressed over a five-year period. More than 4,300 architect's instructions followed fortnightly meetings between the Trust, its architects and consultants. The priority was the support and protection of the building followed by its structural consolidation. However, Uppark was struck by a further disaster. Two workmen were killed when the huge temporary roof supported by scaffolding, which was in place by November 1989, collapsed in a storm on 25 January 1990. This left the interior exposed to the elements for several months

at the most inclement period of the year. The paintwork and gilding of the Saloon, remarkably little damaged by smoke and water, deteriorated visibly. The canopy was rebuilt by August 1990 and restoration began in earnest immediately afterwards. The complexities of the restoration were simplified into 'packages' of work, which were competitively tendered.

Once the shell was secure, the roof structure was rebuilt, supported by massive baulks of oak. The principles of the repairs were applied from the start. The roof had been oak, with slates fixed to wooden laths; the late seventeenth-century cornice supported by carved wooden brackets. So it was again. After analysis to determine their origin, the slates were obtained from the Delabole quarry in Cornwall and were laid in diminishing courses, although, sadly, the larger slates could no longer be supplied.

The Red Drawing Room on the day after the fire

A plasterer at work on the Red Drawing Room ceiling

Several of the boldly carved cornice brackets survived and were replaced; the copies are indistinguishable. An important resource for the restoration was a large photographic archive of the house before the fire. This was the only evidence for the dimensions of the nineteenth-century dormer windows, until a builder involved in a previous restoration telephoned to say that he had one of the originals in store.

The fire was caused by the modern practice of sealing lead joints with a naked flame. The Trust now bans all such 'hot work' so the new lead at Uppark was 'bossed' in the traditional manner by beating it with special wooden mallets. Ready-made sections were formed by 'hot work' in a shed well away from the building and were fitted into place by bossing. The roof was complete by October 1991. The date is marked by one of the handthrown chimneypots inscribed 'Margaret Thatcher resigned as I was making this'. Already, the slates ripple irregularly as they had before, due to the use of wooden laths and beams.

Because the heat and smoke funnelled up through the collapsed roof, the fire had not greatly disturbed the exterior brickwork. Lichens still patinated its surface. Many of the Portland stone lintels and window architraves were, however, considerably

weakened by the heat and had to be replaced. The façades had also been disfigured by melted lead from the roof bouncing off the scaffold planks and spattering the surface of the brick. This lead spatter was dissolved by careful application of heat (the operatives being supervised by fire watchers), and no trace is discernible.

The windows were considerably damaged in the course of the fire. None the less, some of the original mid-eighteenth-century sashes and glass still survive on the west front. Elsewhere, plate glass had been introduced in 1865 and had been replaced in the previous style of smaller panes in the late 1970s. On the south and west fronts, new sash-windows and glass had to be installed yet again. The glass, made in France, is cylinder glass with the reamy imperfections of the traditional process of glassmaking. The glazing bars and exterior woodwork were coated with white lead paint, after permission had been given to use this traditional, but poisonous material, which was preferred because of its durability and attractive weathering qualities. Its constituents and colour derived from analysis of the original treatment of the late seventeenth-century cornice. When the house martins first built their nests under the new cornice in May 1992, Uppark existed again as a house, from the outside at least. The fitting-out of the interior, a much greater challenge, lay ahead.

Despite the collapse of ceiling plasterwork and considerable damage to panelling and carved woodwork, the aim of the interior restoration has been the re-creation of the historic setting for the comparatively undamaged contents in the show rooms. About 90 per cent of these contents had escaped serious harm, much of the remainder was repairable, and only five major pieces of furniture had been totally destroyed by the fire. Given that the surviving furniture retained the patina of age for which Uppark was famous, it was important to consider the tonality of the rooms from the very beginning. Despite their further exposure to the weather after the scaffolding collapse, the Saloon and Dining Room retained much of their original paint and gilding. It was discovered that neither room had been repainted (except for retouching) since c.1815 when Repton decorated them in pure white, which had faded to grey in the Saloon. It was

Gilding the Saloon ceiling

decided to preserve as much as possible of the early paint and gilding and to tone in the new work. The panelling, doorcases and window embrasures in the other rooms also retained paint in good condition. This all had to be protected while the plasterers were plying their wet trade above. Great quantities of decorative woodwork also survived in good condition. The carved wooden chimneypieces in the Tapestry Room and Little Parlour were damaged, but could be restored without extensive repainting or gilding. Long lengths of water-gilded wallpaper fillet and most of the carved pelmets survived intact, as had much of the decorative metalwork: grates, locks, cloak pins, hinges, picture hooks, etc. All these, together with a high proportion of the floorboards and the panelling in the Dining Room, were removed to store after recording their locations, while the remainder was protected *in situ*. The

great work of replastering the Rococo and Neo-classical ceilings could now begin.

The cornices and ceilings were originally executed in a combination of cast and free-hand techniques in lime plaster. The repetitive mouldings of the cornices (and the ribs of the Saloon ceiling) had been cast from wooden moulds. The main body of the ceilings, with their flowing arabesque designs boldly modelled within symmetrical compartments, had been plastered by hand directly on the flat plaster ground. This required the skills of a sculptor and an ability to work quickly and decisively with the rapidly drying stucco. The process was further complicated by the requirement to incorporate salvaged pieces of original plasterwork where this was economically feasible.

The first stage was the selection of plastering companies competent to tender. They had to demonstrate experience in the conservation of historic plaster and an ability to copy it. The craft of free-hand modelling in lime plaster had begun to disappear in the eighteenth century as Neo-classicism increasingly demanded repetitive motifs that could more easily be cast. By the mid-nineteenth century gypsum plaster, with its more precise contours, had replaced lime. Chemical analysis revealed the constituents of the stucco, which was to be used precisely as it had been when the ceilings were first made. In England, no one had attempted to undertake free-hand lime plasterwork on this scale for at least 150 years. Four companies were asked to produce 'exemplars' to prove their abilities. A section of the Red Drawing Room ceiling, combining moulded cornice and free-hand work, was copied. Two of the four were rejected at this stage. Following the tender, the successful firm was subjected to further scrutiny, and individual craftsmen had to undergo trials for several months before being allowed to work in the house.

Having laid the 'flats' of the ceilings on chestnut laths, the decorative plasterwork was begun in the Staircase Hall. The initial process for each room was the laying out of the fragments that had survived the fire. These were fitted, like pieces in a giant jigsaw, on to a cartoon delineating the design. This enabled the exact proportions of each ceiling to be established, and identified the feasibility of re-using fragments. Although the ceilings were recorded photographically, the three-dimensional fragments were vital in establishing the correct degree of relief and volume of each element. The team of free-hand plasterers (ten in all) was put together specially for Uppark – mainly young men and women whose experience ranged from modelling porcelain to sculpture. Several had not worked in plaster before. Their achievement, in emulation of the eighteenth-century stuccadores, is all the more remarkable for their relative inexperience in the medium. A section of each ceiling was carried out in its entirety by an individual, and it is possible to detect the different hands, as was the case in the original.

Meanwhile, in a temporary building where the ceilings had been laid out, cast lime plaster (mainly for the cornices) was being produced from moulds. The plasterers all wore white overalls and caps and the workshop looked like a bakery or an ice-cream factory. Only two sections of cornice (in the

Tapestry Room and Little Parlour) survived *in situ*; the remainder had to be remade, incorporating original pieces. In the Little Parlour the oval Neo-classical reliefs were reconstituted (incorporating surviving fragments) and fitted into the finished ceiling. These would originally have been commissioned separately or bought ready-made. Prior to decoration, it was possible to see precisely how much original plaster had been incorporated in the new ceilings, and comprehensive record photographs were commissioned.

The reconstitution of Uppark's panelling and carved woodwork was next in order of difficulty, given the quality of the original work and the scale of the task. The late seventeenth-century panelling of the Staircase Hall and first floor was virtually destroyed and was remade on the basis of record photographs and fragments, although a large framework section surrounding the door to the Saloon survived and was reused. Fortunately, two small sections of the staircase balustrade served as

One of the writhing serpents on the Saloon doorcases has been left unpainted to show the extent of the new and the original carving

models for the rest and were replaced in their previous positions. One of the Corinthian pilasters, the carved swags and much of the ornate oak cornice and panelling of Repton's Dining Room survived, albeit seriously damaged. Each wall elevation was laid out so that the losses could be quantified. Here, as for all the surviving material, the 'economic test' was applied: if it cost less to restore and re-fit a fragment, then the fragment was reused. This insurance requirement proved an infallible friend to conservation. The huge labour costs of recarving showed again and again that conservation of original material was much the cheaper option. Thus, on hard-headed economic grounds Uppark's restoration had its authenticity guaranteed. In the Dining Room approximately 70 per cent of the woodwork is original. In the other rooms there was a considerable amount of finely carved woodwork to be conserved or replaced. The mid-eighteenth-century carving at Uppark was equivalent in quality to that of the finest contemporary furniture. As with the plaster, the competence of the craftsmen was measured by the submission of copies of an original fragment, in this case a length of carved chair rail. The results were equally remarkable: for example, the missing architrave of one of the Saloon doors, an extraordinary confection of writhing serpents, has been so finely carved as to be indistinguishable from the neighbouring original. Indeed, it was often impossible to prevent the woodcarvers excelling their eighteenth-century predecessors.

Once the plaster and woodwork were completed, and the floorboards returned (many salvaged originals were laid in their previous positions), it was decided to continue the Uppark tradition of minimum redecoration. The paintwork and gilding of the Saloon and Dining Room were conserved, in so far as it was practical to do so, and any losses touched in with paint, or with carefully toned gold leaf. Lead-based paint, specially mixed to an authentic recipe, and incorporating an agent to encourage oxidisation or ageing, was used except for touching up old paint or on new plaster. In the eighteenth century stucco plaster was first painted with porous distemper so that moisture could continue to evaporate. After three years or so, the

Fragments of the original mid-nineteenth-century flock wallpaper (top left) have been restored in the Red Drawing Room. The rest has been reprinted to the same pattern and carefully toned to reproduce the brighter colours of those areas previously protected from light damage by pictures

distemper was washed off and replaced by lead-based oil paint. It was only at this stage that gilding was applied. This would have been impractical at Uppark, and a modern porous casein paint was used which allowed the plaster to breathe and which could be gilded immediately.

Only in the Red Drawing Room had enough original wallpaper survived to be returned to the room after conservation. The salvaged wallpaper was fitted back into place, and new flock paper was made to fill the gaps. The whole was then adeptly toned in, so that the new and the old meld together. Here, and in the other rooms where new wallpaper was made on the basis of surviving fragments, the constituents and manufacture of the original wallpapers were copied. Thus, flock was made from wool rather than synthetics, traditional pigments like cochineal were employed, and the papers were block-printed. In the Tapestry Room, where the paper was originally machine-made, the copy was screen-printed. Upstairs, such was the ferocity of the fire, that there were no surviving fragments. Photographs and Uppark wallpaper samples given to the Victoria & Albert Museum in the 1970s provided sufficient evidence. In one case, a matching wallpaper was found in a Parisian museum.

In the course of digging out the rubble after the fire, some extraordinary discoveries were made. The last area to be excavated was the Staircase Hall, where the heat had been fiercest, to the extent that not a trace was found of a large heavily carved side-table with a marble top. None the less, the framework of the Gothick metal lantern had survived, albeit flattened into fantastic tracery. Its restoration, and that of the gilt-metal French lantern in the Stone Hall, makes it impossible to detect any fire damage whatsover. In the Stone Hall firemen had been powerless to rescue the pair of carved side-tables, *c*.1755, supporting elaborately decorated scagliola tops by Don Petro Belloni. Although one of the stands was virtually destroyed, and one of the tops broken into eight pieces and severely scorched, the pair of tables proved to be repairable without wholesale replacement of the scagliola. Difficult decisions had to be taken in the course of assessing the damage. One of the pair of giltwood pier-glasses in the Red Drawing Room, Rococo masterpieces attributed to Matthias Lock, had been severely damaged by the time it emerged from the burning building. The base section of the frame was charred beyond repair. There was no alternative but to cut it away and re-carve, preserving the charred section for archival purposes. This presented a daunting challenge to the carver, who had both to emulate the flowing lines of the finest carving of its day, and to copy the original as closely as possible.

The salvaged textiles underwent a second stage of repair following the emergency work carried out at Uppark immediately after the fire. The festoon curtains, couched by Lady Meade-Fetherstonhaugh in the 1930s, were repaired in the same style. Where fire damage had created gaps in Lady Meade's 'tramlines', they were filled by couching silk of equal thickness (even though modern silk of the same strength is thinner and therefore more discreet). Netting was applied as an additional protection where necessary. Of particular difficulty was the conservation of the Prince Regent's Bed, which was badly damaged by heat, water and debris. Thanks to Lady Meade-Fetherstonhaugh's preservation of fragments of unused silk in the course of her 1930s repairs, it was possible to fill gaps in the cornice of the bed where the silk has been burned away. Small amounts of new braid had to be re-woven, but the decision was taken early on to preserve as much as possible of the original, even if this was aesthetically questionable. Each element of the bed – canopy, valances, headcloth – had to be considered carefully before work began. Its reinstatement at Uppark is due to the tireless exactitude of the conservators.

The Axminster carpet, dug out of the Red Drawing Room, proved to be the greatest conundrum. Given that a corner had been burned away, one border was severely charred, and there were areas of damage and staining throughout, its future looked uncertain. However, washing greatly improved its overall appearance, and its structure was remarkably sound, so with the minimum re-knotting of damaged or destroyed areas, it has proved possible to re-lay it in the room, where its battered appearance is in accord with the wallpaper.

The return of the contents to the house began in September 1994, after thorough cleaning of the interior and allowing enough time for the newly installed environmental control system reliably to maintain the relative humidity at a conservation level. The main building contract was completed in June 1994 on time and within budget. The costs have been considerable: approximately £20m for the building and the conservation of the contents, which has largely been met from insurance. All the work has been competed for by tender so that economy and value for money could be demonstrated. The highest standards have been maintained by tight control of the quality of workmanship and by vetting of potential tenderers and craftsmen. The size and complexity of the task have tested to the hilt current expertise in building and contents conservation. Nevertheless, Uppark's renaissance and reopening in 1995 was a timely demonstration of the vitality of the National Trust in its centenary year.

CHAPTER SEVEN

TOUR OF THE HOUSE

The Exterior

THE NORTH FRONT

The Portland stone portico of Tuscan columns was erected in *c.*1811–14 by Humphry Repton, who moved the main entrance from the east to the north side of the house at Sir Harry Fetherstonhaugh's request. The island of grass within the turning circle in front of the portico was intended by Repton to be the site of a decorative eye-catcher, a stone 'Lamp post' or a bronzed tripod. However, the money could not be found and Repton advised that it would be better to do nothing rather than install a second-rate centrepiece. The area has lacked a focal point ever since. The stone portico must always have seemed rather an appendage to the brick rear façade of *c.*1690. It was undamaged by the fire, although the brickwork of the main house above and behind the portico has had to be largely replaced. The Venetian window lighting the main

The south front

staircase has been renewed. The front door was painted by Repton 'a quiet not a paper white', and this colour accords rather beautifully with the stuccoed walls, now covered with a vigorous growth of lichen.

THE EAST FRONT

This was the main entrance to the house until the building of Repton's portico. The drive ran through two courtyards flanked by service blocks, whose foundations, with a tunnel leading to the house, were discovered during the recent restoration. Knyff and Kip's view (1695–1701) shows the original arrangement (see p.12).

THE SOUTH FRONT

The south front is the principal façade of the house rebuilt by Lord Grey around 1690. The design has been attributed to William Talman since 1815, and recent research has tended to confirm his responsibility (see p.13). Certain alterations have been made since *c.*1690, notably the replacement within the pediment of the Grey achievement of arms with the Fetherstonhaugh equivalent after 1747. The Grey achievement may still be seen installed in a house in the nearby village of Rake.

The depth of the windows was increased (by lowering them), and the sashes were also replaced *c.*1750. Some of the old seventeenth-century sashes with their broad glazing bars were reused as joists during Sir Matthew's mid-eighteenth-century alterations. In 1865 the eighteenth-century sashes were almost all replaced by four-pane plate-glass windows. A return to the eighteenth-century style of fenestration was made by the Trust in the mid-1970s, and this has been repeated since the fire. The dormer windows were repaired in the renovation of the 1930s, and they, the roof (of Delabole slates laid in diminishing courses) and the wooden cornice of *c.*1690 have been renewed since 1989. However, a few of the carved cornice modillions were salvaged and have been reinstalled.

The brickwork here and on the east and west fronts was remarkably undamaged by the fire. However, some repairs were needed, particularly in the top right-hand corner of this façade, and several stone window architraves were replaced. The sculpted achievement of arms in the pediment survived the fire but had to be detached so that the supporting stonework behind it could be restored.

The Interior

THE NORTH CORRIDOR

Repton built the arcaded North Corridor *c.*1811–14 to provide a link between his new entrance portico and the Staircase Hall of the original house, and it remains as he intended. The Corridor was blackened by smoke, but was otherwise undamaged by the fire, except at the south end adjacent to the Staircase Hall. The original stone colour has been restored since 1989 (it had been overpainted in pink in 1971 to match the Staircase Hall).

The conical metal skylight above the stained glass in the dome is Repton's original, restored and replaced since the fire. The brackets and niches were presumably intended for sculpture, lamps or both.

STAINED GLASS

The stained glass was supplied *c.*1813 by the London firm of Underwood & Doyle. The flower motif of the lunettes has a curiously art nouveau appearance by contrast to the Neo-classical borders.

HEATING

The two 'hot water pedestals . . . panelled in front and at both ends with ornamental open work and pilasters at corners' with 'polished marble tops' were supplied in 1835 by William Summers, Stove Manufacturers, of New Bond Street.

DOOR

The elaborately nailed crimson felt door is a copy of the original.

FURNITURE

The pair of padouk-wood (Burmese red wood) benches c.1815, and the set of mahogany oval-backed hall chairs c.1790, bear the Fetherstonhaugh arms.

CERAMICS

The two blue-and-white cabbage-leaf jugs are Worcester, *c.*1775.

The pair of blue-and-white ewers is Japanese, *c.*1660–80. They belong to a small group of both oriental and European blue-and-white which could have been in the Tankerville house of *c.*1690.

THE SERVERY

Constructed by Repton *c.*1812–13, concurrently with his alterations to the adjoining Dining Room and designed to communicate with the kitchen below and after *c.*1815 with the separate kitchen pavilion via the basement passages. Until the Kitchen (see p.77) was returned to the house after 1895, food had to be carried along these passages on wooden trollies equipped with charcoal-heated hot-cupboards, and up the service staircase. It could then be put down here on the side-table, the covers removed and the final touches made, before being brought to table. If there was any delay, a further hot-cupboard and a 'wine sarcophagus' (listed here in 1874 and probably identical with the mahogany cabinets now in the Dining Room) kept food and drink at the right temperatures.

In the 1880s breakfast was taken at 9, for which the dairy maid would dish up here 'all my butter and fancy breads and butters, creams, Devonshire cream etc., on lovely silver and china plates, butter dishes, cheese stands, folded serviettes'.

The Servery was undamaged by the fire, but suffered from smoke and water and had to be redecorated afterwards.

STAINED GLASS

Repton took particular trouble with the stained glass and its illumination. In January 1813 he informed Sir Harry that he had 'unpacked the Stained Glass' at Underwood's London shop. He described the 'few figures in clear obscure on a white panel . . . taken from a pure classic model – as my son [John Adey Repton] has made some sketches from the marbles imported from Athens by

Lord Elgin'. (The Elgin Marbles were first exhibited in London in 1807 and purchased for the British Museum in 1816.) J. A. Repton's drawings were translated into stained glass by W. Doyle, who signed and dated each panel in 1813. The 'center piece' of the otherwise wholly Neo-classical window is a late sixteenth-century Flemish roundel depicting a banqueting scene – an appropriate subject, as Repton intended the window to be seen from the Dining Room, 'by day and candlelight'. He wrote that 'the effect will be magic as all the light may proceed from this window from Argand lamps properly adjusted from behind'. (These were colza oil lamps invented by the Swiss Ami Argand, and first demonstrated in 1783.)

HEATING

ABOVE SIDE-TABLE:

The '3 handsome trellis-pattern brass Ventilators' were installed in 1835 as part of a hot-air heating system.

The brazier would have been filled with charcoal to provide heating. The first plumbed heating system was installed at Uppark in 1835.

FURNITURE

The massive white and gold carved side-table was one of a pair (the other, then in the Staircase Hall, was destroyed in the fire). They were probably one of Sir Matthew's earlier commissions (ie soon after 1747) and intended for the north wall of the Saloon where Repton's bookcases have stood since *c.*1815.

The pair of candelabra is French, *c.*1800, and is in the style usually associated with Pierre-Philippe Thomire (1751–1843), the greatest *fondeur-ciseleur* (metal-chaser) of the Empire period. This is probably the pair bought in Paris in 1803 from M. Carais.

ON SIDE TABLE:

The clock in an elaborate Boulle case with ormolu mounts is French, early eighteenth-century. Its movement is English, having been replaced by Thwaites & Reed of Clerkenwell, a firm founded in 1817. Thwaites & Reed billed Sir Harry for repairs to two French clocks in 1846.

The ormolu reproductions of the Marly Horses are signed by Pierre François Feuchière (1737–1823). The original marble statues, larger than life-size, were made (1740–5) by Guillaume Coustou the Elder (1677–1746) for the royal park of Marly, outside Paris. In 1794 the originals were set up in the Place de la Concorde and are now in the Louvre.

THE DINING ROOM

Here Sir Harry and his friends enjoyed the famous cuisine of his French chef, Moget. After dinner and once the ladies had withdrawn, a screen allowed gentlemen to make discreet use of the chamberpot kept in the Servery.

This was originally two rooms, in 1705 called 'My Lords Bedchamber' and 'The Parlor Next'. The bedroom was 'hung with tapestry and Guilded Leather', while the bed-hangings were of 'Sad Colour and Green Damask trimmed with Scarlet Lace'. The window curtains were green, as were the curtains in the adjoining room, which was also hung with gilt leather. By 1722 the rooms were described as the 'Red Damask and Alcove Rooms', and contained 'red jappan carved and Silver'd furniture'.

It is unclear when the two rooms became a single dining-room, but Repton appears to have been wholly responsible for the present arrangement, which dates from 1812–13.

The room was severely damaged in 1989. As throughout the ground floor, the ceiling (here plain) collapsed and has had to be restored.

PANELLING

The panelling, the fluted Corinthian pilasters and the cornice were once thought to be seventeenth-century, but the panel mouldings are not comparable to the seventeenth-century bolection mouldings elsewhere in the house, and the white and gold colour scheme is the first to have been applied. Indeed, apart from subsequent touching-up and post-fire replacements, the paint and gilding dates from soon after 1812–13, when Thomas and James Hughes were paid for plasterwork associated with Repton's alterations. Following the fire the surviving panelling (about 70 per cent) was dismantled and returned to the room after conservation. The original paint and gilding have been preserved and matched where they are missing.

CHIMNEYPIECE

The marble fireplace was presumably installed during Repton's alterations.

The Dining Room

TEXTILES

The curtains were relatively undamaged by the fire and could have been part of Repton's original décor. He recommended that the 'yellow curtains' should be enhanced by 'blue velvet drapery at the top'. Hangings of 'Garter Blue velvet with gold fringe' were also suggested as a foil for 'Gold Plate' in the arched recesses.

PICTURES

They are still hung as Sir Harry arranged them. The panelling between the windows, and above and to the right of the fireplace, retains the shadows of the picture-hang recorded in an early ninetenth-century set of diagrams. The picture rail and brass hooks are original. These and the replacement silk cords here, and elsewhere in the house, were probably originally introduced by Sir Harry.

WINDOW WALL:

? ENGLISH, ? 1598
? *Catherine Fetherston* (d.1622)
Panel

? ENGLISH, ? 1598
? *Cuthbert Fetherston* (1537–1615)
Panel

Usher and crier to Elizabeth I and James I, he built Hassingbrooke Hall in Essex and was the grandfather of Sir Heneage Fetherstone, 1st Bt (see p.57). Husband of the above. The identification of both is traditional, but the likeness of Cuthbert accords with the sculpted image on his tomb in St Dunstan's-in-the-West, London.

FIREPLACE WALL:

JOSEPH VERNET (1714–89)
The Four Times of Day
Signed and dated 1751
Vernet's Italianate marine paintings were extremely popular with British visitors to Rome in the 1750s. This set was commissioned in 1750 by Sir Matthew Fetherstonhaugh's brother-in-law and fellow Grand Tourist, Benjamin Lethieullier, together with a pair of *River Landscapes* (Little Parlour), and evidently bequeathed to Uppark. Sir Matthew was so taken with them that he ordered a further four, and then two more, but Vernet seems to have passed on the commission as one for copies of the *Four Times of Day* to his former assistant, Charles-François Lacroix de Marseille.

OVER FIREPLACE:

CORNELIS ENGELSZEN (1575–1642/3)
Kitchen Interior with Christ in the House of Mary and Martha
Signed with monogram
Modern still-life painting began in the Low Countries with artists like Beuckelaer and Aertsen, who often coupled kitchen scenes with this episode in *Luke* (x, 38–42), in which Martha, the archetype of the busy cook, chides her sister Mary Magdalen for sitting in apparent idleness listening to the words of Christ.

SCULPTURE

Sir Harry conceived the room as a testament to his political sympathies, incorporating busts of Napoleon and Whig notabilities on brackets above mirrored alcoves (originally intended to incorporate racks for the display of plate). The concept may have derived from a similar set of Whig portrait busts placed by the Prince of Wales in the vestibule of Carlton House.

GEORGE GARRARD (1760–1826)
Garrard began his career as a horse painter before turning to animal sculpture and then portrait busts. He sculpted both the busts and the overdoor plaques, which are all of plaster painted to resemble bronze. The 6th Duke of Bedford employed Garrard at Woburn and was a close friend of Sir Harry, so Garrard was probably recommended personally for the Uppark commission. The Uppark overdoors are most comparable to those by Garrard in the entrance hall at Southill, Bedfordshire, c.1805.

SOUTH WALL:

Napoleon (1769–1821)
Dated 1 December 1802 (original)
Fox (see below) and many of his Whig followers were initially sympathetic to Napoleon during his rise to power.

William Battine, FRS (1765–1836)
Prosperous lawyer, occasional writer and leading local Whig politician. The son of Lord Tankerville's agent, he was a friend of Sir Harry, and like him, also of the Prince of Wales in his youth. Original (dated 1 October 1805).

NORTH WALL:

Charles James Fox (1749–1806)
Copy of the original (dated 28 July 1805), destroyed in the fire. Leader of the Whig party in the Commons and principal opponent of Pitt the Younger. He also supported the Prince of Wales against his father.

A mirrored niche in the Dining Room. The recarved head at the top right has been left unpainted

Francis, 5th Duke of Bedford (1765–1802)
Copy of the original (dated 27 July 1805), destroyed in the fire. Like Sir Harry, the 5th Duke was a friend of the Prince of Wales and of Fox, who delivered the eulogy in the Commons at his death.

OVERDOORS:

Stag at Bay
'The Wanton Courser'
Both have had to be remade since the fire, although some fragments of the originals (dated 1 and 30 November 1804) have survived. The subjects are taken from Pope's Homer.

FURNITURE

The dining-table is *c*.1770 and could therefore be that upon which Emma Hart is said to have danced naked for Sir Harry and his friends in 1780–1.

The leather upholstered dining-chairs and the massive armchair are *c*.1760.

BETWEEN WINDOWS:

The pair of mahogany cabinets is *c*.1775 and was probably in the Servery in 1874 (see p.48).

The bronze and ormolu (gilt-bronze) wall sconces are *c*.1815.

TEXTILES

The carpet is a mid-nineteenth-century 'Turkey' of English manufacture.

SILVER

The collection of plate at Uppark was once extensive, including functional and display silver and silver-gilt engraved with the Fetherstonhaugh arms. Much was sold in 1972, including dining-room, library and chamber silver belonging to Sir Matthew, some of which was acquired by the Trust. Sir Harry added considerably to his father's collection by purchasing a pair of two-branch dining-room candelabra (1783), a set of twelve silver dinner plates (1778), in addition to his father's large set of the 1760s, and items such as an elaborate Neo-classical cruet stand (1808). In the 1820s he purchased ornamental plate in the neo-Rococo and neo-Renaissance styles – a development of taste comparable to that of the Prince Regent. In 1874 there was no less than 12,032oz of silver for use in the Dining Room.

ON DINING-TABLE:

JAMES YOUNG (active 1749–88)
Silver-gilt racing cup
Engraved 'The Prince's Cup Uppark 1785'
The cresting is in the form of Prince of Wales's feathers issuing from a crown. The oval medallions represent Neptune and Bacchus. The cup was won by Sir Harry riding his own horse 'Epaminondas' against the Prince of Wales's 'Nottingham' on the Downs below the house. Young also supplied Sir Harry with oval dessert dishes in 1779.

ON MANTELPIECE:

Silver-gilt cup
Engraved 'The Lewis Cup' (Lewes Races)
Dated 1779 and made by Carter, Smith & Sharp.

CERAMICS

ON DINING-TABLE:

A Chinese armorial dinner service, *c*.1765, with the arms of Sir Matthew Fetherstonhaugh impaling those of his wife, Sarah Lethieullier.

ON MARBLE SIDEBOARDS:

Four large Japanese Imari vases and covers, three with finials formed as Shishi (Buddhist lion) on rock-work, the fourth with a pheasant, *c*.1700.

THE STONE HALL

This stone-flagged room was designated 'the Stone Hall' in 1705 and, until Repton's construction of the north portico (*c*.1815), was the day-to-day entrance to the house. In 1705 it was furnished simply with 'fourteen maps, two Tables [and] Seven Cane Chairs'. During restoration, evidence was discovered of a wooden floor, which may have belonged to the late seventeenth-century house.

The room was refitted in the mid-eighteenth century, when the simple cornice was inserted. As far as we know, the ceiling has always been plain.

CHIMNEYPIECE

The white marble fireplace dates from Sir Matthew's redecoration and is presumably by Thomas Carter (who supplied those in the Saloon) to the design of James Paine. It features children garlanding a goat flanked by sphinxes and upturned cornucopiae, all carved with great accomplishment.

DECORATION

The green paint (which is partly original – see the remnants to the right of the fireplace) replaced a dark pink in the nineteenth century (its emerald green pigment was invented in 1814). Previously, there were two blue schemes; the earliest layer is stone colour.

LANTERN

*The Louis XVI ormolu (gilt-bronze) hall lantern, c.*1785, is in the manner of Pierre Gouthière (*maître* in 1758, d.1813), who made superlative mounts for furniture and porcelain. This great rarity was possibly supplied to Sir Harry by the dealer Dominique Daguerre, from whom the Prince of Wales made numerous acquisitions for Carlton House. Severely damaged in the fire (and retrieved three weeks afterwards), it now bears no sign of its ordeal.

TEXTILES

Luckily, a fragment of the *wool damask curtains* of *c.*1830–40 survived the fire, and copies have been hung. The pelmets are replacements, incorporating fragments of the originals.

PICTURES

They were removed before the fire took hold (and have been rehung largely as before). The overmantel picture is in its *c.*1815 position, the Vermeulens slightly lower, as they then had pictures below them.

FIREPLACE WALL, OVER DOOR:

BENJAMIN WEST, PRA (1738–1820)
*? Joshua Iremonger IV (c.*1744–1817)
Probably of the elder son of Sarah, Lady Fetherstonhaugh's half-brother Joshua III, of Wherwell Priory, Hampshire. It is a slightly revised repetition of West's earlier portrait of the same sitter (private collection, USA), painted in the early 1770s. Sarah may have wanted an image of her nephew at Uppark, to accompany the copy of West's contemporary and similarly sized portrait of her son Harry (Staircase Hall), who is likewise dressed in a vaguely 'artistic' version of contemporary costume.

OVER FIREPLACE:

FRANS SNYDERS (1579–1657)
A Larder with Dead Game
An unusual vertical composition by this artist, datable to the 1640s.

The marble chimneypiece in the Stone Hall

RIGHT OF FIREPLACE, ABOVE:

WILLIAM SHAW (active 1758–72)
A Horse in a Landscape

BELOW:

CORNELIUS JOHNSON (?1593–1664)
An Old Woman
Panel
Signed with monogram

WEST WALL (OPPOSITE WINDOW), ABOVE LEFT:

VAL PRINSEP, RA (1836–1904)
Admiral of the Fleet Sir Richard Meade, 4th Earl of Clanwilliam, GCB, GCMG (1832–1907)
Having entered the Royal Navy in 1845, he rose to command the Fleet in 1895. He was severely wounded in a small boat action at Canton in 1857. His son (below) was left Uppark in 1931.

BELOW:

WILLIAM SHAW (active 1758–72)
A Hunter held by its Owner
In 1766 Matthew Fetherstonhaugh paid Shaw £27 6s for two pictures.

OVER DOOR:

Sir OSWALD BIRLEY (1880–1952)
Admiral the Hon. Sir Herbert Meade-Fetherstonhaugh, KCVO, CB, DSO (1875–1964)
Signed and dated 1940
The third son of the 4th Earl of Clanwilliam (above)

and like him a distinguished seaman, commanding the light cruiser *Royalist* at the battle of Jutland in 1916. He took the name of Fetherstonhaugh on succeeding to Uppark in 1931.

ABOVE RIGHT:

GEORGE FREDERICK WATTS, OM, RA (1817–1904)
Richard Meade, 3rd Earl of Clanwilliam (1795–1879)
Board
In his youth he was a leading diplomat, serving with the Foreign Secretary Lord Castlereagh at the Congress of Vienna in 1814–15 and then in the Foreign Office from 1817 to 1823. For the last 31 years of his life he was Captain of Deal Castle. Grandfather of the previous sitter and father of the 4th Earl.

BELOW:

JAN FYT (1611–61)
Still-life with Fruit
Signed

WALL OPPOSITE FIREPLACE, FLANKING DOOR:

JACOB XAVIER VERMOELEN (c.1714–84)
Still-lifes with Game (pair)
One signed and dated at Rome 1751, and therefore probably a Grand Tour purchase by Sir Matthew.

OVER DOOR:

THOMAS PHILLIPS, RA (1770–1845)
William Battine, FRS (1765–1836)
Dated 1803
For biography, see p.51.

FURNITURE

FLANKING DOOR TO STAIRCASE HALL:

The pair of scagliola-topped side-tables was purchased by Sir Matthew, who commissioned the scagliola slabs, possibly in 1750, from Don Petro Belloni (active 1740–60), who signed and dated one of them in 1754. Don Petro was assistant to Don Enrico Hugford (1697–1771), Abbot of the monastery of Vallombrosa near Florence, who was principally responsible for refining the art of scagliola from 'being merely a cheap and easily worked substitute for marble and mosaic'. Scagliola is a plaster made of pulverised selenite (gypsum) painted, fired and polished to resemble, in this case, *pietra dura* or inlaid marble. Apart from the Uppark pair, there are only five documented table-tops by Belloni (dated 1750 and 1756), all commissioned by friends of Sir Matthew who were travelling in Italy at the same time (see p.21). The white and gold carved frames were probably made or supplied by John Bladwell.

Both tables were severely damaged by the fire. The base of the left-hand (south) table is a modern replacement incorporating original fragments, and the top was broken into eight pieces, the scagliola layer being shattered into over 100 pieces. The other table too was broken in half, but otherwise is substantially intact. The greater proportion of the wooden base is original. The bases were originally entirely gilded; the white paint was probably applied c.1815.

The white and gold carved frames for the scagliola-topped side-tables in the Stone Hall were commissioned by Sir Matthew, probably from John Bladwell (photographed before the fire)

The white and gilt overmantel mirror in the Rococo style is *c*.1750. Burnt sections have had to be replaced and the glass renewed, but it is substantially original.

The set of mahogany chairs, some with nineteenth-century embroidered upholstery, is *c*.1750.

BETWEEN WINDOWS:

The English pier-glass and table, both *c*.1750 but not a pair, were destroyed in the fire and have been replaced by copies. However, the table retains its inlaid marble top (a replacement of *c*.1800), and is similar in design to the architectural side-tables at Fetherstonhaugh House, illustrated in Paine's *Works* (1767).

CERAMICS

ON CHIMNEYPIECE:

Three Chinese mugs painted with the arms of Fetherstonhaugh impaling Lethieullier, *c*.1765.

A pair of Chinese blue-and-white sprinkler vases, Kangxi, *c*.1700.

A pair of Delft blue-and-white flower vases, early eighteenth-century.

ON TABLES:

Two Chinese blue-and-white shaped oval dishes and two circular dishes with the Fetherstonhaugh and Lethieullier arms, *c*.1765.

THE LITTLE PARLOUR

This sunny room has always been favoured by the ladies of Uppark. It was Lady Meade-Fetherston-haugh's sitting-room, and before 1893 it was the principal scene of the 'shrunken routines' to which Wells referred when recalling the last years of Frances Fetherstonhaugh and Ann Sutherland: 'When there was no company, they spent whole days in the corner parlour . . . between reading and slumber and caressing their two pet dogs.'

It is another room that has preserved its name since 1705, when it contained ten cane chairs, four tables including two of 'Large ovall' shape, and two 'prospect Glasses' (presumably oblong mirrors).

The Neo-classical cornice, ceiling, panelled dado and doorcases were added *c*.1770, and are attributable to James Paine.

The carved-wood head of Bacchus on the Little Parlour chimneypiece

The Little Parlour was demolished soon after 3am on 31 August 1989, when a chimneystack crashed through the ceiling, plunging the room (including the chandelier) through the floor into the basement. Although the floorboards could not be salvaged, three out of five pelmet boxes and even elements of the chandelier were saved.

CHIMNEYPIECE

The wooden chimneypiece, carved with the head of Bacchus, vine tendrils and grapes, predates the principal decoration, having been installed *c*.1750, probably by James Paine during his first campaign of work.

WALL-COVERINGS

The fire revealed oak panelling of *c*.1690 painted grey-blue beneath later wall-coverings. Its bolection mouldings had been removed in order to hang wallpaper, presumably around 1750, when the chimneypiece was installed. At that time the room was hung with painted Chinese wallpaper, depicting birds roosting among flowering branches (a section was discovered after the fire). This was papered over with a green distemper diaper-patterned wallpaper, concurrently with the *c*.1770 redecoration.

CEILING

The ceiling medallions framed by garlands hanging from ribbons perhaps by Joseph Rose, are reminiscent of Paine's grand staircase (1770–6) at Wardour Castle, Wiltshire. They were made separately and fitted into the ceiling. All, bar one, were retrieved more or less intact after the fire – the missing sections have been remade. The remainder of the ceiling was executed free-hand *in situ*, by reference to fragments and photographs. The cornice, in cast lime stucco, has been remade – the section to the left of the fireplace survived the fire.

DECORATION

The room has been repainted according to evidence of an early nineteenth-century scheme (John Fowler had modified it slightly when the room was redecorated in 1970). The green of the walls was originally applied post-1814 and matches the adjoining Stone Hall. The pelmet boxes and the white picking-out of the wallpaper fillet, as well as the partial gilding of the chimneypiece, were also early nineteenth-century alterations, possibly concurrent with Repton's work elsewhere in the house.

TEXTILES

The red silk damask festoon curtains, of a pattern usually called 'Amberley', are the first of a long set, possibly eighteenth-century in date, also hung in three other principal rooms. Two of the Little Parlour curtains survived the fire (one had been torn in half) and have been returned after conservation; the other two are copies.

PICTURES

In rehanging the pictures, the arrangement recorded in the early nineteenth century has been emulated in so far as that has proved possible. The pictures are hung with red silken rope (copying the original) suspended from floral ormolu hooks of *c*.1815.

WEST WALL (FACING WINDOWS):

OVER DOOR TO SALOON:

POMPEO BATONI (1708–87)
Sir Matthew Fetherstonhaugh, 1st Bt, MP
(1714–74)
Signed and dated 1751
After buying Uppark in 1747, he and his wife Sarah (below) spent the years 1749–51 on a Grand Tour of

One of the Neo-classical plasterwork medallions on the Little Parlour ceiling

France and Italy, accompanied by his brother Utrick and his future wife Katherine, and Sarah's brother Benjamin Lethieullier and half-brother Lascelles Iremonger. In Rome they were all painted (in three cases twice) by Batoni, and so were among his earliest and most important British patrons. He holds a wreath of figs and cherries in his right hand, a wreath of corn in his left.

ABOVE:

JOSEPH VERNET (1714–89)
Two River Landscapes (pair)
Signed and dated 1751
Commissioned in Rome by Benjamin Lethieullier at the same time as Vernet's *Four Times of Day* in the Dining Room.

BELOW LEFT:

By or after HENDRICK VAN STEENWYCK the Younger (*c*.1580–*c*.1649)
A Church Interior
Panel
The architecture and figures may be by different hands. Steenwyck the Younger settled in London *c*.1617–*c*.1637.

BELOW RIGHT:

Attributed to LAMBERT DE HONDT the Elder
(before 1620–65)
A Cavalry Skirmish
The Teniers signature is false. De Hondt was a
battle-painter from Mechelen who worked in this
manner.

FIREPLACE WALL, ABOVE LEFT:

CHARLES-FRANÇOIS LACROIX DE MARSEILLE
(c.1700–82) after JOSEPH VERNET (1714–89)
Harbour Scene: Evening
Signed and dated 1751
One of three excellent contemporary copies by a
former assistant of Vernet, after the paintings in
the Dining Room, perhaps commissioned by Sir
Matthew when Vernet himself was unable to produce original compositions (see Dining Room). The
fourth copy was lost in the fire.

BELOW:

After CAVALIERE D'ARPINO (1568–1640)
The Agony in the Garden
The original is in the Allen Memorial Art Gallery,
Oberlin, Ohio.

OVER FIREPLACE:

CHARLES-FRANÇOIS LACROIX DE MARSEILLE
(c.1700–82) after JOSEPH VERNET (1714–89)
Seaport by Moonlight: Night
Signed and dated 1751
Copy of the picture in the Dining Room.

OVER DOOR:

POMPEO BATONI (1708–87)
Sarah Lethieullier, Lady Fetherstonhaugh (1722–88)
Signed and dated 1751
The daughter of Christopher Lethieullier and Sarah
Lascelles, she married Matthew Fetherstonhaugh
(above) in 1746.

ABOVE PIER-GLASSES (BETWEEN WINDOWS):

ENGLISH, late seventeenth-century
Sir Henry Fetherston, 2nd Bt (1654–1746)
Eldest son of Sir Heneage (above), he left the bulk of
his £400,000 fortune to his Northumbrian kinsman
Matthew Fetherstonhaugh.

ENGLISH, late seventeenth-century
? Sir Heneage Fetherston, 1st Bt (1627–1711)
Eldest son of Henry Fetherston of Hassingbrook
Hall, Essex, and father of Sir Henry Fetherston

(below), according to a label on the back, but the
date of the picture (c.1680s) and the age of the sitter
cast doubt on this identification.

FURNITURE

The chandelier was probably supplied for the room
c.1770–4 and is a slightly smaller version of the
chandelier in the Red Drawing Room. Both are
attributed to Christopher Haedy (active 1769–85),
who had premises in London and Bath. In 1775, at
Church Street, Bath, he advertised chandeliers
'ornamented with festoons of entire paste, etc. etc.'.
The group of chandeliers attributed to Haedy are
distinctive for their solid stems and for their festoons
of solid glass ['paste'] strung between notched spires.
Since the appalling damage wreaked by the fire, the
Uppark chandeliers have had to be extensively
restored, although the maximum number of original pieces has been reused.

The chandelier tassels, matching the pair in the Red
Drawing Room, are probably those supplied in
1836 by Edward Bailey of Mount Street, London.
Some of the woven silk cords were renewed in
1933, when the chandeliers were rehung by the
seaman rigger of the Royal Yacht *Victoria and
Albert*. The present cords are recent replacements
copying Bailey's original pattern.

The pair of giltwood pier-tables with carved acanthus
decoration, supporting black and white marble
tops, was presumably supplied for these positions,
c.1770–4. They are in the style of Robert Adam
(1728–92).

The pair of giltwood pier-glasses, en suite with the
overmantel mirror, was probably installed c.1815,
when Sir Harry was employing Repton to make
alterations. The pier-glasses were evidently designed so that pictures could be hung above, an
arrangement that is recorded in the picture-hanging
diagrams of c.1815.

The white and gilt armchairs closely resemble French
chairs of the period, c.1770, and are in the tradition
of similar chairs by Thomas Chippendale (1718–79)
supplied to Nostell Priory and Harewood in Yorkshire, 1768–75.

The green and white painted beechwood caned chairs are
from a long set of c.1770, again in the French style.

The veneered satinwood bonheur du jour, or lady's
writing-table, is English in the most refined French
taste of c.1770. It also illustrates the transition

between Rococo and Neo-classical decoration; while its legs are cabriole, its superstructure is entirely rectilinear and the marquetry, which incorporates the Fetherstonhaugh antelope crest, is unfalteringly Neo-classical. It is attributed to John Cobb (*c*.1715–78).

The mahogany breakfast table, incorporating an open fretwork cupboard, is *c*.1765.

The mahogany tripod table is *c*.1760.

BY SALOON DOOR:

The small mahogany corner cupboard on a tripod stand is *c*.1760.

IN CENTRE OF WEST WALL:

The black japanned 'pagoda' cabinet inset with Chinese lacquer and Florentine *pietra dura* panels and with ivories after the Antique, is an exotic hybrid combining chinoiserie with Italian spoils of Sir Matthew's Grand Tour. It is comparable to designs published by John Mayhew (1736–1811) and William Ince (d.1804) (*Universal System of Household Furniture*, 1762, plates XLVIII–XLIX) and by Thomas Chippendale (*The Gentleman and Cabinet-Maker's Director*, 1754). Its date is therefore *c*.1755–60 and it was probably commissioned for the Little Parlour, to complement the Chinese wallpaper. Its maker is unknown. Subsequently, it was in the Prince Regent's Room, where the royal guest was said to have tethered his dog to one of its legs.

ON CHIMNEYBREAST:

The ormolu sconces are from a set of four (see p.71).

TEXTILES

The Persian carpet is late nineteenth-century.

CERAMICS

ON CHIMNEYPIECE:

A Paris vase, bearing the monogram and portrait of Sir Harry's friend, Francis, 5th Duke of Bedford, *c*.1795.

A pair of Chinese Dehua blanc-de-chine figures of Buddhist lions forming incense holders, late seventeenth-century.

A pair of Chinese white figures of parrots, early eighteenth-century.

A Dehua blanc-de-chine group of Guanyin with child and attendants, late seventeenth-century.

Five Chinese famille rose figures of kneeling boys, Qianlong, *c*.1770.

Two Chinese white figures of Liuhai with his three-legged tadpole, Qianlong, *c*.1770.

A pair of Sceaux faience oval pierced baskets, marked 'SX', *c*.1760.

An early eighteenth-century Chinese powder blue vase and cover with Louis XVI ormolu finial.

Two Chinese blue-and-white two-handled cups and saucers, late eighteenth-century.

A pair of Chinese famille rose saucer dishes with pierced blue borders, Qianlong, *c*.1760.

THE SALOON

In the Tankerville house this was the formal entrance hall, giving access to the Staircase Hall, through an originally taller door in the north wall, and to ranges of apartments on the east and west. In 1705 it was furnished with 'Eighteen Dutch Chaires two long mats' and called the 'Greate Hall'; it was even taller, taking in the mezzanine floor above, which now contains the Print Room. In the 1722 inventory it was described as the 'Marble Hall', which may suggest that it was stone-flagged at that time.

Around 1770 Sir Matthew created the present Saloon, one of the most beautiful of its date in Britain, probably to designs by Paine. This room, more than any other, expresses the Trust's aim of perpetuating the substance and spirit of Uppark before the fire.

CHIMNEYPIECES

The original fireplaces flanked the doorway on the north wall. The present monumental chimneypieces on the west and east walls are by Thomas Carter the Elder (d.1756). The central reliefs, illustrating the stories of *Romulus and Remus* (west) and *Androcles and the Lion* are set in Siena marble friezes and flanked by terms with heads of classical worthies such as Homer (west, right) and Hesiod (east, right). Stylistically, they seem to be earlier (*c*.1750) than the rest and it may be that they represent a first stage in Sir Matthew's alteration of the original Great Hall. Nevertheless they incorporate elements typical of Paine, notably the central pediments, which he adopted from William Kent.

The Saloon

CEILING

The ceiling combines a central coffered oval in the Palladian style with flowing arabesque ornament in the surrounding panels and coving that anticipates Robert Adam. Compartmented ceilings of this kind were a Paine trademark. There are comparable examples by him at Sandbeck Park, Yorkshire, Brocket Hall, Hertfordshire, and Shrubland Park, Suffolk.

PICTURE FRAMES AND DOOR CAPITALS

The gilt plaster ribbons and crossed palms (above the overmantel state portraits) are also typical of Paine. The most curious (and virtuoso) element of the Uppark Saloon, the door architrave capitals in the form of snakes, cannot be paralleled in his work. However, an equally eccentric animal detail was published in his *Works* (1783): pairs of squirrels placed back-to-back as capitals. The top right and lower left-hand corners of the south-west doorcase have been left unpainted to show the extent of the original and restored carving.

DECORATION

The Saloon was redecorated in white (now faded to grey) and gold by Humphry Repton, when he introduced the bookcases flanking the north door in *c*.1814. When they were moved after the fire, decorative plasterwork was revealed behind. This showed that the previous colour of the walls was green with the raised plasterwork relieved in a stony white; the ceiling was pink and white. The original scheme was a darker green relieved by white for the walls with the ceiling compartments in alternating lavender and blue, again with white picking out.

The plaster, paint and gilding of the walls and part of the cornice remained largely undamaged by the fire, despite the collapse of the ceiling. Even though the Saloon was open to the elements for several months following the destruction of scaffolding in January 1990, enough of Repton's decoration survived to allow for the matching-in of new plasterwork and woodwork.

PICTURES

With its fixed plaster frames for paintings, the Saloon remains one of the few places where an eighteenth-century picture-hang survives intact. The brass picture rails on the fireplace walls are probably early nineteenth-century (compare the similar rails in Repton's Dining Room). The Batonis with Zuccarellis beneath were recorded in these positions in the early nineteenth century.

EAST (NEAR) WALL, OVER DOOR:

MICHAEL DAHL (1656/9–1743)
? Christopher Lethieullier (1676–1736)
Of Belmont, Middlesex. Married in 1721, as his second wife, Sarah Lascelles, who bore him two sons and a daughter, Sarah, who married Matthew Fetherstonhaugh in 1746. Director of the Bank of England.

OVER FIREPLACE:

NATHANIEL DANCE, RA (1735–1811)
George III (1738–1820)
These portraits of the Royal Academy's patron and his consort (opposite) were shown at its first exhibition, which was held in premises provided by the King in Somerset House in 1769. Dance was one of the younger foundation RAs, who had painted a similar full-length portrait of the King's brother, the Duke of York, in 1764 and an early piece of British Neo-classicism, *Timon of Athens*, the following year for the King (both Royal Collection). The Uppark portraits were perhaps acquired by Sir Matthew at the time Dance was painting his son (see below) in the early 1770s.

POMPEO BATONI (1708–87)
Meekness
One of Batoni's most exquisite works. A young woman cradling a lamb traditionally personifies the third Beatitude from the Sermon on the Mount: 'Blessed are the meek: for they shall inherit the earth' (*Matthew*, v, 4). With its pendant (opposite), perhaps commissioned by, or given to, Sir Matthew's brother, the Rev. Utrick Fetherstonhaugh, who was a member of the party in Rome.

FRANCESCO ZUCCARELLI, RA (1702–88)
An Italian Landscape
Probably acquired by Sir Matthew, perhaps in Venice through Consul Joseph Smith, who found a ready market for such gently classicising landscapes among British visitors. This success encouraged Zuccarelli to settle in England (1752–62, *c*.1764/5–71), where he became a founder member of the Royal Academy.

The Romulus and Remus plaque, carved by Thomas Carter c.1750, on the west chimneypiece in the Saloon

WALL OPPOSITE WINDOW, RIGHT OF DOOR:

LUCA GIORDANO (1632–1705)
Parable of the Prodigal Son: The Son receiving his Portion
The son leans across the table to his father, while another figure on the left counts out his inheritance. The first in Giordano's cycle of six scenes, possibly painted in Florence in the early 1680s and probably acquired by Sir Matthew on his Grand Tour. The gospel narrative (*Luke*, xv, 11–32) is relatively brief, allowing artists considerable latitude.

OVER DOOR:

NATHANIEL DANCE, RA (1735–1811)
Sir Harry Fetherstonhaugh (1754–1846) as a Boy
Signed
For biography, see p.66. Dance had studied with Batoni while in Rome from 1754 to 1765, which must have recommended him to the Fetherstonhaughs; this portrait of their only son was clearly inspired by Batoni's 'hunting' portraits of them in the Red Drawing Room (see p.65).

LEFT OF DOOR:

LUCA GIORDANO (1632–1705)
Parable of the Prodigal Son: Riotous Living
The son squanders his inheritance in feasting and riotous living.

WEST (FAR) WALL:

POMPEO BATONI (1708–87)
Purity of Heart
Signed and dated 1752

Personification of the sixth Beatitude: 'Blessed are the pure in heart: for they shall see God' (*Matthew*, v, 8). The lily symbolises purity, the dove the Holy Ghost. Pendant to *Meekness* (opposite).

FRANCESCO ZUCCARELLI, RA (1702–88)
An Italian Landscape

OVER FIREPLACE:

NATHANIEL DANCE, RA (1735–1811)
Queen Charlotte (1744–1818)
Pendant to the portrait of her consort opposite.

OVER DOOR:

MICHAEL DAHL (1656/9–1743)
Sarah Lascelles, Mrs Lethieullier
Daughter of Edward Lascelles of Stoke Newington, she married, firstly, in 1717, Joshua Iremonger II, to whom she bore two sons, Joshua III and Lascelles; her second husband (1721) was Christopher Lethieullier, by whom she had a daughter, Sarah, who married Sir Matthew, and two sons, Benjamin and Christopher.

FURNITURE

BETWEEN WINDOWS:

The plain gilt pier-glasses were part of the original furnishings of the room. They were relatively undamaged by the fire, though some of the glass has been replaced.

BENEATH:

The marble pier-tables supported by cast bronze consoles in the form of serpents were presumably introduced by Repton *c*.1815, given their similarity to the bronze consoles in the Dining Room. They are French, dating from the Consulate and Empire periods (*c*.1800–14).

The set of four pedestals is attributed to Louis XIV's *ébéniste*, André-Charles Boulle (1642–1732), who gave his name to this style of metal inlaid wood and tortoiseshell furniture. This model of pedestal closely follows a design by Boulle published in his *Nouveaux Desseins de Meubles et Ouvrages de Bronze et de Menuiserie*.

The set of eight giltwood armchairs upholstered in tapestry (the matching sofa is reupholstered), *c*.1755–60, has been attributed to John Bladwell, but could equally have been supplied by the weaver and cabinetmaker Paul Saunders (1722–71), to whom Sir Matthew paid £336d for 'Tapestry' in 1761. Their distinctive wide tapering backs and other characteristics are close to designs for 'French Chairs' illustrated in Chippendale's *Director* (1754)

The doorcase on the north wall of the Saloon

and Ince and Mayhew's *Universal System of Household Furniture* (1762). The cover of one of the chairs is signed Danthon, the name of a family of Huguenot weavers who were working in London by 1693. The subjects are taken from Aesop's *Fables*, a 1666 edition of which, illustrated by Francis Barlow, was frequently used as a basis for upholstery.

AGAINST EAST AND WEST WALLS (BESIDE CHIMNEYPIECES):

The pair of giltwood side-tables with carved masks in the frieze and marble tops was presumably among Sir Matthew's first purchases for Uppark, *c*.1747–9.

ON LEFT-HAND SIDE OF ROOM:

The pair of large upholstered sofas on mahogany bases is *c*.1755–60. They were re-covered by John Fowler *c*.1970.

The padoukwood wine table on the tripod cabriole legs is *c*.1755–60.

The ormolu-mounted Régence (1715–23) bureau plat, or writing-table, is veneered in ebony and inlaid with Boulle work and tortoiseshell. It was presumably one of Sir Harry's purchases, and, with the Boulle pedestals, is an important survival from the Uppark collection of French furniture, which, until *c*.1910, also included pieces by Riesener and Carlin. It supports a late Louis XV *cartonnier* (bookcase), of *c*.1770, and an Empire clock of *c*.1800, signed by Charles-Guillaume Manière (*maître*, 1778; d.1810). The clock case, of gilded and patinated bronze, is in the form of Apollo, holding a lyre and flambeau, leaning on an altar. It was probably bought by Sir Harry in 1803 from Martin-Eloy Lignereux (1750/51–1809), a Parisian dealer associated with Dominique Daguerre (see p.53).

The French ormolu chandelier is late eighteenth-century or early nineteenth-century in the style of the *Régence* period (1715–23). Although it crashed to the floor when the ceiling collapsed, it was remarkably undamaged to the extent that no regilding was necessary.

FLANKING EAST (NEAR) FIREPLACE:

The pair of fire-screens is English, early nineteenth-century. One of the pair of banners was deliberately left untouched by Lady Meade-Fetherstonhaugh to illustrate the previous condition of the textiles that she repaired in the 1930s and after the war.

CERAMICS

ON CHIMNEYPIECES:

A set of four early eighteenth-century Chinese powder blue vases with Empire ormolu mounts. Bought in 1819.

ON FLOOR BESIDE GILT SIDE-TABLES:

A pair of large Chinese powder blue vases, mid-eighteenth-century.

ON ONE PAIR OF PEDESTALS:

A pair of Sèvres (First Empire) vases Medicis, painted in grisaille with scenes from the life of the Indian prince Tippoo Sahib (1749–99).

FLANKING CENTRAL DOOR:

A pair of large Sèvres ormolu-mounted vases painted with *Danaë* (after Correggio's painting in the Borghese Gallery, Rome) and the *Venus of Urbino* (after Titian's painting in the Uffizi, Florence).

A small white and gilt Paris supper dish and cover with hot water compartment, *c.*1790.

TEXTILES

The carpet is of an early nineteenth-century Axminster type, probably purchased by Sir Harry.

THE RED DRAWING ROOM

This is the first, largest and most public of the sequence of rooms along the west front of the house. In 1705 it was called the 'Greate Parlor', which suggests that it was being used as a family sitting- and eating-room. At that time it contained 'five paire of Window Curtains' (so there was the same number of windows) and 'Eighteen Wallnut tree Chaires' with 'one folding wallnut Tree Table'. The walnut chair in the south-west corner of the room could be a survivor from this set. There is evidence that this was a panelled room hung with tapestry or leather (but this is not substantiated by the early inventories).

The room was redecorated for Sir Matthew either just before or soon after his return from the Continent in 1751, when the plasterwork ceiling, box cornice, doorcases and chimneypiece were put up, probably to designs by Paine. Around 1815, when Repton's new Dining Room at the opposite corner of the house would have been finished, it was called the 'Great Drawing Room' and has been used as such ever since.

Despite the severe damage wrought by the fire, the survival rate is considerable.

WALLPAPER

The fire revealed that the mid-eighteenth-century room also had red flock wallpaper, but of a different design. It was apparently similar to the 'Flower'd Red paper' originally hung in Paine's Cabinet at Felbrigg in Norfolk. The present wallpaper is partly new but incorporates salvaged remnants of a flock probably supplied in 1851 or 1859 (see on the fireplace wall and opposite and between the windows).

DOORCASE

It is interesting to note how awkwardly the mid-eighteenth-century doorcase in the corner right of the fireplace was squeezed in – similar doorcases may be seen in the following rooms, where the new architraves could only be fitted with difficulty into the late seventeenth-century openings.

CEILING

Apart from the wallpaper, the elaborate ceiling incorporates a high proportion of salvaged material – notably the human masks at either end and large amounts of the fruit and flowers sculpted in lime stucco. That these are indistinguishable from the new work shows how skilfully the plasterers have employed the identical technique of free-hand lime plaster. Before the fire, the ceiling retained late eighteenth- or early nineteenth-century Prussian blue and white paint, discoloured by age. Originally, the whole ceiling was white.

PICTURES

Apart from the Neapolitan landscapes beneath the Giordanos and the large landscape to the right of the fireplace, all the pictures hang in their early nineteenth-century and possibly earlier positions.

SOUTH WALL (OVER PIER-GLASS):

DUTCH, early seventeenth-century
Mother and Son
Panel
The awkward composition suggests it has been cut down from a larger picture. Recorded in this position *c.*1815.

The Red Drawing Room

*The Red Drawing Room
chimneypiece*

SOUTH-WEST CORNER (BETWEEN WINDOWS):

FRANZ DE PAULA FERG (1689–1737)
Landscape with a Village on a Hill
Landscape with a Castle on a Hill
Austrian by birth, Ferg came to England in about
1718, and turned out quantities of small, precious
landscapes in the Netherlandish manner.

LONG WALL OPPOSITE WINDOWS, OVER DOOR
(RIGHT):

POMPEO BATONI (1708–87)
Sarah Lethieullier, Lady Fetherstonhaugh (1722–88)
Signed and dated 1751
Painted the same year as Batoni's other portrait of
her, in the Little Parlour (see which, for biography).
Portrayed in this case as the huntress Diana, with
crescent moon, bow and hunting dog, to match the
conception of her husband as a hunter (below).

ABOVE:

LUCA GIORDANO (1632–1705)
Parable of the Prodigal Son: The Penitent Swineherd
The poverty-stricken son is reduced to herding
swine and prays for forgiveness.

*Parable of the Prodigal Son: The Prodigal Driven out by
his Employers*

BELOW:

TOMMASO RUIZ (active 1740s)
From a set of five Neapolitan views probably
bought by Sir Matthew on his Grand Tour.

Nothing is known of Ruiz, whose name suggests a
Spanish origin. One was destroyed in 1989.

The Bay of Naples, with the Chiaia, seen from Posillipo
View towards Capo Miseno and Procida
The Bay of Naples, looking towards Posillipo
*The Bay of Naples, with Vesuvius and the Sorrentine
Peninsula*
All signed

CENTRE:

After GERARD DOU (1613–75)
A Fiddler at a Window
Panel
Bears signature and date 1665
The original, dated 1665, is in the Dresden
Gemäldegalerie.

OVER DOOR (LEFT):

POMPEO BATONI (1708–87)
Benjamin Lethieullier, MP (1728/9–97)
Signed and dated 1752
Of Belmont, Middlesex, and Middleton, Hampshire. The elder son of Christopher Lethieullier,
and brother of Sarah Lethieullier, who married Sir
Matthew in 1746. He accompanied the Fetherstonhaughs to Rome, where he was painted, like his
brother-in-law (below), as a boar-hunter.

FIREPLACE WALL, ABOVE RIGHT:

HERMAN VAN SWANEVELDT (*c.*1600–55)
An Evening Landscape
Signed and dated 1649
An Italianate scene painted in Paris by a Dutchman, of the kind popular with the English in the eighteenth century. Probably acquired by Sir Matthew during his Grand Tour.

BELOW:

HIERONYMUS JANSSENS (1624–93)
A Picture Gallery with Fashionable Visitors
By the 1660s, the probable date of this picture, David Teniers the Younger had established a fashion for realistic descriptions of such picture galleries. Janssens harks back to an earlier Flemish tradition of more allegorical depictions: the contrast between the precious objects on the table at the left

and the *Last Judgement* in the foreground points to the ultimate vanity of earthly pleasures.

OVER FIREPLACE:

POMPEO BATONI (1708–87)
Sir Harry Fetherstonhaugh, 2nd Bt, MP (1754–1846)
Signed and dated 1776
The only child of Sir Matthew Fetherstonhaugh and Sarah Lethieullier. Like his parents 25 years before, he made the Grand Tour, in 1775–6, and, like them, was painted in Rome by Batoni, in a similar form, but on a grander scale. The mastiff's collar bears the middle seven letters of its master's surname. In his youth Sir Harry was a friend of the Prince of Wales and an energetic member of fashionable society, but around 1810 he became estranged from the Prince. It was not until 1825 that he took a wife, Mary Ann Bullock, a young woman who worked in the Uppark dairy.

OVER DOOR:

POMPEO BATONI (1708–87)
Sir Matthew Fetherstonhaugh, 1st Bt, MP (1714–74)
Signed and dated 1751
Portrayed with archaic boar spear, perhaps as the hunter Endymion, loved by Diana, although Batoni was more interested in painting the luxuriously fur-trimmed hunting coat than in literal-minded allegory.

LEFT OF DOOR TO LITTLE DRAWING ROOM:

SARAH LETHIEULLIER, LADY FETHERSTONHAUGH (1722–88)

ABOVE:

A 'West Indian little black Monkey' with birds, butterflies and flowers
Watercolour on parchment, initialled and dated 1757

BELOW:

A 'Carolina brown squirrel' with birds, butterflies and flowers
Watercolour on parchment, initialled and dated 1754
The keys, in Sarah Fetherstonhaugh's hand, list the animals and plants she portrayed 'in their natural size'. The mid-eighteenth-century plan of the garden includes a menagerie.

(Left) Detail of one of a pair of Rococo pier-glasses in the Red Drawing Room

Ceiling plasterwork in the Red Drawing Room

FURNITURE

BETWEEN WINDOWS:

The pair of elaborately carved giltwood pier-glasses, c.1750, is attributed to Matthias Lock (c.1710–65). The wild-men and water nymphs, bearing baskets of fruit and flowers, are similar to a design in his *Six Sconces* (1744). These masterpieces of the French-inspired English Rococo are also closely comparable to the pier-glasses published as plate CLXX in Chippendale's *Director* (1763). Both glasses were severely damaged by the fire: the left-hand (south) frame had to have its bottom section cut off and recarved, and the cresting of the right-hand (north) mirror is also new. Both have been almost entirely regilded and reglazed (with replacement nine-teenth-century glass). They may have been originally painted white, or parcel gilt.

BENEATH:

The pair of commodes, of c.1760–5, incorporating panels of Chinese lacquer, is attributed to Pierre Langlois (active 1759–81), a Parisian *ébéniste* who was practising in London by 1759. Commodes of this outstanding quality were 'more intended to furnish and adorn than for real use'. The Uppark pair is possibly unique among the group attributed to Langlois, in that the gilded mounts are partly executed in carved wood.

ON SOUTH WALL:

The gilded pier-glass is English, c.1770.

BENEATH:

The carved giltwood pier-table with a marble top is in the Rococo style of c.1750.

The mahogany writing-table, c.1790, the top edged with tiers of drawers, is of a type known as a 'Carlton House' table. By family tradition, it was a gift to Sir Harry from the Prince of Wales, who rebuilt Carlton House from c.1784.

The rosewood grand piano, a replacement for the Broadwood piano destroyed in the fire, was also made by Broadwood, c.1880–5. On loan from Capt. and Mrs Sierks.

The chandelier, the larger of two supplied c.1770–4, is attributed to Christopher Haedy (see p.57).

The straight-backed sofa, upholstered in red damask, is c.1800.

BY FIREPLACE:

The pair of wing armchairs and the stool, upholstered in red damask, are c.1755.

The small writing-table on cabriole legs with a fire-screen incorporated in the top is c.1770.

ON RIGHT (EAST) WALL:

The mahogany architect's table is c.1770.

The mahogany side-chairs, upholstered in red damask, are c.1770.

The giltwood armchairs covered in pink velvet (faded to brown) are English c.1770 in the French style.

ABOVE CHIMNEYPIECE:

The tortoiseshell cane belonged to Sir Harry, whose portrait hangs above. The knob of gold and mother-of-pearl is embossed with a figure of Cupid. (On loan from the Victoria & Albert Museum.)

The pair of ormolu sconces is French of the *Régence* period (1715–23).

TEXTILES

The carpet is an Axminster of c.1800. The pattern of the central field is identical to carpets at Woburn Abbey and Osterley Park, although the borders are different. After the fire, the carpet was presumed lost, but it emerged from the wreckage three days later. Despite being charred and covered in sludge, its structure was intact, although the matching hearth rug was beyond repair. The most damaged areas were reknotted and, although fragile, it has been possible to return the carpet to the room.

CERAMICS

A Sèvres ormolu-mounted vase formed from a *seau à bouteille* (wine-cooler) with *beau bleu* ground. Possibly bought in 1819.

*A pair of Chinese famille rose basins, c.*1765. These would originally have been fitted into mahogany washstands and have had matching bottles.

IN FRONT OF FIREPLACE:

A Delft blue-and-white flower vase in four sections, *c.*1690. It was reassembled in the 1960s and is one of only four complete vases of this type still in existence. It may have been acquired by the builder of the house.

A Sèvres two-handled ormolu-mounted vase, one side decorated with a pastoral scene, the other with a shipwreck. Bought by Sir Harry in 1819.

A Japanese Imari tureen, cover and stand, the cover pierced, early eighteenth-century.

A Sèvres plate with *beau bleu* border, painted by Xhrouet, *c.*1765.

A Sèvres white hard paste vase du roi with gilt relief decoration, *c.*1776.

A pair of Sèvres blue shaped shallow bowls. Bought in 1819.

A pair of Sèvres ormolu-mounted vases on porphyry bases, painted with classical and pastoral scenes, eighteenth-century. The ormolu mounts were added in the early nineteenth century.

A large Sèvres bowl painted with city views on a *beau bleu* ground, 1782, gilded by Le Bel. Probably bought in 1819.

*A pair of Crown Derby ice pails, covers and liners, c.*1790.

A pair of beau bleu Sèvres vases à oreilles (with ear-shaped handles) with gilt arabesques. Possibly bought in 1819.

ON ARCHITECT'S TABLE:

A large Sèvres bowl with sprays of flowers on a white ground.

THE LITTLE DRAWING ROOM

In 1705 this was the 'Withdrawing Room', to which the family and their more favoured guests could retire from the 'Greate Parlor'. It was more richly decorated than the preceding room and was hung 'with Fine Guilt Leather'. The window curtains were of 'fine Damask', and the twelve 'Black Chaires' were upholstered *en suite*.

The ceiling, woodwork and pelmets are all elements of Sir Matthew's remodelling, *c.*1750. The room assumed its present name by at least *c.*1815. By 1874 it had assumed the additional role of dressing-room to the adjoining Tapestry Bed-room, and was furnished with a washstand, toilet set and bidet.

The fire damage was considerable: both the ceiling and floor fell into the basement. The floorboards are, therefore, mostly new.

CHIMNEYPIECE

*The marble chimneypiece, c.*1755, is in Paine's style, but may be a later insertion. The wooden fireplace in the Tapestry Room would accord more closely with the ceiling decoration here. The central panel depicts Aesop's fable of the Fox and the Crane. The crane can drink from the pitcher, but not the fox, which had earlier expected the crane to drink from a flat bowl. The moral is: 'Do as you would be done by'.

WALLPAPER

The wallpaper (copied since the fire from fragments of the original) was probably the 'Satin Flock' paper hung in 1859.

CEILING

The ceiling incorporates several original elements, including the central Apollo mask and one of the armorial cartouches (nearest the Red Drawing Room door) with the antelope crest of the Fether-stonhaughs. As in the adjoining Red Drawing Room, the blue and white scheme was probably first applied in the eighteenth century, but the original colour was plain white.

Apollo mask and sunburst on the Little Drawing Room ceiling

PICTURES

FIREPLACE WALL, OVER DOOR:

POMPEO BATONI (1708–87)
Katherine Durnford, Mrs Fetherstonhaugh
Signed and dated 1751
Sixth daughter of Dr Durnford, Vicar of Harting, and wife of the Rev. Utrick Fetherstonhaugh (below), younger brother of Sir Matthew, whom she and her future husband joined on the family's Grand Tour in 1749–51.

OVER FIREPLACE:

CHARLES-FRANÇOIS LACROIX DE MARSEILLE (*c.*1700–82) after JOSEPH VERNET (1714–89)
Storm: Midday
Signed and dated 1751
Copy of the picture in the Dining Room.

FRANCESCO ZUCCARELLI, RA (1702–88)
Italian Landscape with Boy Piping
Italian Landscape with Children Fishing

WALL OPPOSITE WINDOW:

LUCA GIORDANO (1632–1705)
The Parable of the Prodigal Son: The Fatted Calf
The father (centre) forgives his son and provides a feast in his honour.

POMPEO BATONI (1708–87)
The Rev. Utrick Fetherstonhaugh (1717/18–88)
Signed and dated 1751
Younger brother of Sir Matthew and husband of Katherine Durnford (above); he was appointed Rector of Harting in 1757. The arrows and crook hung up on the tree, the lyre, and the gesture of conducting music, appear to be allusions to the god

69

'Received Home by his Father', from the Parable of the Prodigal Son cycle by Luca Giordano (Little Drawing Room). The set was probably acquired by Sir Matthew Fetherstonhaugh during his Grand Tour

Apollo, brother of Diana, in which guise Batoni painted his sister-in-law (Red Drawing Room). He later acted as tutor to his nephew, Sir Harry, accompanying him on his Grand Tour.

WALL OPPOSITE FIREPLACE:

LUCA GIORDANO (1632–1705)
The Parable of the Prodigal Son: Received Home by his Father
Having squandered his inheritance in wild living, the prodigal son returns home, telling his father, 'I have sinned against heaven, and in thy sight, and am no more worthy to be called thy son'. The poses of the father and son seem to have been based on an engraving by Pietro Testa which also inspired Murillo (Beit collection, Russborough, Co. Wicklow).

OVER DOOR:

POMPEO BATONI (1708–87)
Lascelles Raymond Iremonger (1718/19–93)
Signed and dated 1751
Second son of Sarah Lascelles, posthumously by her first husband Joshua Iremonger II, and thus half-brother of Sarah, Lady Fetherstonhaugh. He accompanied the family's Grand Tour and is painted holding wreaths of corn and roses, very much as in Batoni's contemporary portraits of the Fetherstonhaughs in the Little Parlour. He was a member of the Earl of Charlemont's set in Rome.

FURNITURE

BETWEEN WINDOWS:

The giltwood pier-glass of *c*.1755 is one of the finest in the house. In Chinese taste, and still markedly Rococo, it can be linked most closely to a design of *c*.1752 published by Matthias Lock, reprinted as plate 4 in the 1769 reissue of his *A New Book of Ornaments for Looking Glass Frames*. A masterpiece of virtuoso carving, it was almost undamaged by the fire and retains its original glass.

IN CENTRE OF ROOM:

The mahogany writing-table is *c*.1790.

The pair of carved mahogany card-tables is *c*.1755.

The mahogany chairs, c.1750, on cabriole legs ending in scrolled toes, are part of a set which retains its original green silk upholstery.

The mahogany writing-desk on stand is *c*.1755.

ON FAR WALL:

The lacquer cabinet, japanned in imitation of Chinese lacquer, is English, *c*.1755–60.

ON CHIMNEYBREAST:

The ormolu sconces with backplates in the form of ram's heads, *c*.1765, may perhaps be connected with a payment by Sir Matthew to Matthew Boulton (1728–1809), the leading English supplier of decorative ormolu and Sheffield plate.

TEXTILES

The festoon curtains are probably the 'mauve and crimson figured stripe Merino damask' curtains provided by Charles Hindley of Oxford Street in 1852.

CERAMICS

ON CHIMNEYPIECE:

A set of three large Sèvres vases and covers with ormolu swags. Bought in 1819.

A pot-pourri vase and cover, probably assembled by E. H. Baldock (1777–1845). It is formed of an eighteenth-century Sèvres chamberpot, from which the handle has been removed and the scars hidden under the ormolu. The Sèvres base, dated 1761, originally supported a biscuit figure of Cupid, hence the Latin inscription from Virgil: *Omnia Vincit Amor* ('Love conquers all'). The turquoise seated putto with a birdcage on the top is French, *c*.1825.

THE TAPESTRY BEDROOM

This was the 'Best Bedchamber' in 1705, the bed being hung with damask 'Trimed with Gold Lace'. Seven chairs were upholstered to match and the window curtains were white with a 'Sprigd' pattern.

Most of the woodwork was installed by Sir Matthew in the mid-eighteenth century. Sir Harry is said to have used this as his bedroom. The 1874 inventory probably records Sir Harry's arrangement, when the room was furnished much as it is today, but with a different bed, flanked by pot-cupboards. By 1910 it was a sitting-room, and by 1931, when it became the Admiral's room, it was considered 'cold and unlived in', although the fire was the only one on this floor to be lit regularly. (It was doused each night with a watering can.) A television was installed here on the Admiral's 80th birthday in 1956.

CHIMNEYPIECE

The carved wooden fireplace, with its Apollo mask, looks earlier (*c*.1747–9) than the rest of the woodwork, and may originally have belonged in the Little Drawing Room with its plaster Apollo in the centre of the ceiling.

CEILING

For some reason, the ceiling here is plain. There are elaborate ceiling designs in Paine's style which may have been intended for use here.

WALLPAPER

The present wallpaper is a copy of the original roller-printed paper (now silk-screened) of *c*.1840–50, at the earliest.

PICTURES

OVER FIREPLACE:

JOSEPH FRANCIS GILBERT (1792–1835)
South Harting
Signed and dated 1834
The village of South Harting, in the valley below Uppark, formed part of the estate. On the edge of the village are the pumping house and Engine Pond, from which water was pumped up to Uppark.

The Tapestry Bedroom

WALL OPPOSITE WINDOW, OVER DOOR:

ENGLISH, early eighteenth century
Matthew Fetherstonhaugh the Elder (c.1660–1762)
Oval
Twice Mayor of Newcastle, who reputedly lived to be over 100. Husband of Sarah Brown (below) and father of Sir Matthew Fetherstonhaugh, 1st Bt, of Uppark.

WALL OPPOSITE FIREPLACE, OVER DOOR:

ENGLISH, early eighteenth-century
Sarah Brown, Mrs Fetherstonhaugh (d.1767)
Oval
Daughter of Robert Brown, she married Matthew Fetherstonhaugh the Elder in 1710, to whom she left a large fortune bequeathed by her only brother.

FURNITURE

The mahogany-framed bed, upholstered in partly embroidered silk damask, is a composite piece put together after *c.*1760 (the earliest date of the mahogany bedposts). The canopy, tester cloth, head-cloth and bedspread belonged to an earlier bed or beds of *c.*1720–30 and are, by tradition, part of the Lethieullier collection brought to Uppark by Sarah Lethieullier after her marriage in 1746. The giltwood putti standing at the corners of the canopy are of seventeenth-century Continental origin and may have been added in the early nineteenth century.

Until recently, the bed stood upstairs in the Prince Regent's Room and was presumably used by the Prince in 1784 and 1785. In 1796 he invited himself to stay and requested of Sir Harry 'my old Bed at Up Park'.

The bed was severely damaged by heat and water in the course of the fire, although it was found to be intact on the following morning. Its repair has been extremely complicated.

BETWEEN WINDOWS:

The giltwood pier-glass is one of the large number of Rococo examples supplied to Uppark in *c.*1755. It was largely undamaged by the fire. By comparison to similar pieces at Felbrigg, it is attributable to John Bladwell.

BENEATH:

The serpentine mahogany chest-of-drawers is *c.*1755.

The parcel gilt overmantel mirror of *c.*1755 has had burnt sections replaced and has been reglazed.

FLANKING BED:

The pair of mahogany pot-cupboards is c.1785.

AT FOOT OF BED:

The couch or day-bed is *c.*1790.

The mahogany cheval dressing-glass with brass candle branches is *c.*1800.

TEXTILES

The pair of festoon curtains (and the giltwood pelmets) are replacements.

The Flemish early eighteenth-century tapestries inspired by David Teniers the Younger (1610–90), depict harvest and vintage scenes. That behind the bed, *The Village Fair*, is signed 'V. Leyniers'. Urbain (*c.*1674–1747) and his brother Daniel (1669–1728) Leyniers produced most of their Teniers tapestries between 1712 and 1734. The tapestries were recently returned to Uppark through the good offices of the American National Bank and Trust Company of Chicago which purchased them in 1972, and have been refixed in their original positions. This was made possible by the generosity of an anonymous donor, who provided the money to buy the Bank a replacement set. The tapestries were nailed to the wall with upholstery pins when the wallpaper was first applied in *c.*1840–50, at the earliest. The other two, *The Return from the Harvest* and *The Village Fair*, are generally associated with the workshop of Peter van den Hecke (d.1752).

CERAMICS

A garniture of three Sèvres jardinières, dated 1774 and bearing the coats of arms of the Dauphin and Dauphine of France (probably executed by the Sèvres gilder Vincent). These are probably the set bought by Marie-Antoinette in October 1773. The shape was probably designed by Jean-Claude Duplessis the elder (active 1745/8–74). Further decoration of cupids on clouds on rose Pompadour grounds was added in the 1820s, probably by a decorator working for Edward Holmes Baldock (1777–1845).

ON POT-CUPBOARDS FLANKING BED:

*A Paris ewer and basin, c.*1780. Possibly bought by Sir Harry in 1819.

A creamware veilleuse (food warmer), probably Derby, Cockpit Hill factory, *c.*1775.

ON CHEST OF DRAWERS:

A blue-and-white Lambeth Delft pill slab with the arms and motto of the Society of Apothecaries, late seventeenth-century. These were probably used as signs for display in a pharmacy window.

THE FLOWER ROOM

In 1705 this was 'the Closet Next [the Best Bedchamber]' – the room in which whoever was using the bedroom could wash and dress; it was then 'hung with Striped Camelet' (woollen cloth). The panelling (completely destroyed by the fire) must therefore have been later, like the fire surround, which could be by Paine of *c.*1750, and the mahogany chest-of-drawers (*c.*1780, and copied since the fire), inserted beneath the window.

Until the fire, this room was the only one to retain the thick glazing bars of the original late seventeenth-century sash-windows (renewed in the mid-eighteenth century by Sir Matthew). In 1874 it was the bathroom and WC, and it later housed the first Uppark telephone.

PICTURES

As well as a photograph of Sir Harry's widow (née Bullock), the drawings shown here include a depiction of the coat of arms created for her and portraits of Col. Keith Turnour-Fetherstonhaugh and his wife.

CERAMICS

ON CHEST IN WINDOW:

A Chinese blue-and-white fluted oval deep dish, mid-eighteenth-century.
A Copeland washing service.

THE STAIRCASE HALL

Until the fire, the panelling and staircase woodwork were as erected by Lord Tankerville *c.*1690. Now, they are copies, although two original sections of the stair survived (the newel post at the bottom and a section of the balustrade on the first-floor landing). Fragments of the panelling enabled the precise copying of the original.

The Staircase Hall was probably remodelled by

Paine *c*.1750, when the walls and ceiling were replastered and the Venetian window inserted. All these elements are closely comparable to Paine's Staircase Hall at Wadworth Hall, Yorkshire, also *c*.1750. Several fragments of the ceiling survived the fire to be fitted back into place, and the panelled wall plasterwork remained undamaged *in situ*.

Here, the fire was at its fiercest. In the lower hall, a marble-topped side-table (its pair is in the Servery) disappeared without trace. The canvas of a large painting introduced by Admiral Meade-Fetherstonhaugh hanging above the upper flight of stairs was flayed off its stretcher by the heat.

DECORATION

The Staircase Hall was first painted stone colour, then a creamy yellow. The present pink and white colour scheme was first introduced in the nineteenth century. The pink could be the 'Peach Blossom Colour' applied in 1826, when the Venetian window, brackets and busts were 'Twice flatted Dead White' and the balustrade was 'Grained in Imitation of New Oak'. The balustrade was stripped by Lady Meade-Fetherstonhaugh in 1933–4, who found in the process that it had originally been white and gold, although this was not substantiated during recent investigation of the paintwork. A bordered stair carpet 'in rich colours' was laid between 1835 and 1840, but although the guides for stair-rods are still in place, it had disappeared long before the fire.

PICTURES

WALL OPPOSITE ENTRANCE:

PIETER TILLEMANS (1684–1734)
View of Uppark
This shows the house built by the 1st Earl of Tankerville *c*.1690 and the similar laundry and stable blocks in their original position to the east of the main building.

PIETER TILLEMANS (1684–1734)
View on the Downs near Uppark
South Harting can be seen in the valley. Harting Place, the ancient seat of the owners of the Harting estate, still stands next to the church. The huntsmen wear the blue and silver livery of the local Charlton hunt. Both pictures were probably painted in the 1720s for Charles, 2nd Earl of Tankerville of the second creation, who sold Uppark in 1747.

OVER DOOR TO SALOON:

Studio of BENJAMIN WEST, PRA (1738–1820)
Sir Harry Fetherstonhaugh, 2nd Bt (1754–1846) as a boy
A copy of the portrait painted on his departure from Eton, where he was a pupil from 1766 to 1771. It had become customary for Eton boys to present 'leaving portraits' to the headmaster of the school, where the original still hangs.

WEST WALL:

WILLIAM HOARE OF BATH (1707–92)
Sir Matthew Fetherstonhaugh, 1st Bt, MP (1714–74)
Pastel
Sir Matthew visited Bath in 1753, when these portraits were probably painted.

WILLIAM HOARE OF BATH (1707–92)
Sarah Lethieullier, Lady Fetherstonhaugh (1725–88)
Pendant to the above. She is in 'Tyrolean' costume, in imitation of the 'fancy' pastels of Rosalba Carriera – and perhaps in anticipation of the Grand Tour about to take her across the Alps.

STAIRCASE WALL:

JOHN BOULTBEE (1733–1812)
Prophet and Surprise
Signed
Racehorses belonging to Sir Matthew Fetherstonhaugh.

SAMUEL DRUMMOND, ARA (1765–1844)
The Battle of Trafalgar, 21 October 1805
After running away to sea and serving in the Navy for several years, Drummond taught himself to paint, specialising in maritime history pictures. This loan from the National Maritime Museum replaces the Admiral's picture of the same subject by François Musin (1820–81), destroyed in the fire (see above).

SCULPTURE

Plaster busts on brackets are a Paine characteristic. The originals (copies after the Antique lost in the fire) may have been the busts supplied to Sir Matthew by John Cheere in 1759, and if so, provide a terminal date for the Staircase Hall.

FURNITURE

The large parcel gilt side-table is a copy of the table of *c*.1747–9 destroyed in the fire. Previously painted black, probably in mourning for Sir Harry's death

*The Staircase
Hall ceiling*

in 1846 (by tradition, it supported his coffin), the copy corresponds exactly to its original pendant (in the Servery, see p.49).

ON SIDE-TABLE:

The clock in an elaborate Boulle case with ormolu mounts is French, early eighteenth-century. Its movement is English, having been replaced by Thwaites & Reed of Clerkenwell, a firm founded in 1817. Thwaites & Reed billed Sir Harry for repairs to two French clocks in 1846.

The ormolu reproductions of the Marly Horses are signed by Pierre-François Feuchière (1737–1823). The original marble statues, larger than life-size, were made (1740–5) by Guillaume Coustou the Elder (1677–1746) for the royal park of Marly, outside Paris. In 1794 the originals were set up in the Place de la Concorde and are now in the Louvre.

*The pair of giltwood mirrors, c.*1755, may be attributed to John Bladwell, who supplied so much furniture to Sir Matthew. One of the bevelled glass plates is original; the other was replaced by Lady Meade-Fetherstonhaugh in 1933 after she had found that the mirror had 'fallen and smashed the glass'.

The mahogany chairs with distinctive interlaced ribbon splats are similar to designs for 'Hall' and 'Parlour' chairs published in Matthias Darly's *Second Book of Chairs* (*c.*1751) and Robert Manwaring's *The Chair-Maker's Guide* (1766).

The hanging lantern in Gothick style, *c.*1760, is similar to a 'Lanthorn . . . an hexagon in the Gothic Taste' published in Ince and Mayhew's *The Universal System of Household Furniture* (1762). Flattened by the collapse of the ceiling, and discovered in the rubble a month after the fire, the lantern has made a virtually complete recovery. The elaborate chain also survived the fire. The glass was broken, but fragments allowed the plates to be re-created to the same profile. The replacement eighteenth-century smoke cowl is from Chevening, Kent.

CERAMICS

ON LARGE SIDE-TABLE:

A pair of Chinese late Ming blue-and-white bottles, mid-eighteenth-century.

A pair of Chinese blue-and-white ginger jars, mid-eighteenth-century.

A pair of Chinese powder blue ginger jars (the covers not matching), early eighteenth-century.

Visitors ascend the stairs and enter the Print Room via another short flight of stairs in the centre of the landing. The Print Room is opened on a limited basis only.

THE PRINT ROOM

Part of the mezzanine floor inserted *c*.1770 during the construction of the Saloon below, the Print Room was totally destroyed by the fire. Fortunately, the prints and their straw-coloured backing paper had been removed for conservation beforehand. Admiral Meade-Fetherstonhaugh used this room as a dressing-room from 1931, and is said to have scanned the Solent with a telescope, while commenting upon his colleagues' seamanship.

MIRROR

The carved mirror, carefully stored in a packing case inside the room, was incinerated and has been replaced by a copy. This mirror, with its carved dolphins, may have been part of the original decoration of the room before it was hung with prints. It corresponds to sections of a wooden fireplace which was removed from the old estate office in 1978. Both are consistent with the style of James Paine in the late 1760s and early 1770s. The chimneypieces in the adjoining rooms must also have been designed by Paine.

PRINTS

The practice of pasting engravings to backing paper (usually straw-coloured, blue or green) and arranging them like a miniature picture gallery with paper frames, decorative masks and ribbons may have originated in England *c*.1750 and was also popular on the Continent. Engravers such as Francis Vivarès (1709–80) and Thomas Major (1720–99) supplied

The Print Room before the fire: the bed, the mirror and the other furniture were destroyed

the decorative elements, which, in theory at least, could be applied by amateurs. In 1774 Sir Matthew paid £5 15s to 'Mrs. Vivaro for Prints'.

The Uppark room consists mainly of prints after Italian, Flemish and Spanish Old Masters. These include a series of engravings depicting scenes of witchcraft and alchemy after David Teniers the Younger (1610–90). The latest in date is Fisher's engraving (1762) of Sir Joshua Reynolds's *Garrick between Tragedy and Comedy* (centre, top register, east wall).

FLOWERS

The cut-out watercolours of flowers in terracotta pots around the skirting were added later, probably in the early nineteenth century.

From the Staircase Hall, visitors retrace their steps through Repton's North Corridor and turn right towards the Servery. Before reaching the Servery they descend the Service Stairs to the left.

Above the head of the stairs is an eighteenth-century dial with a float-operated pointer that indicated the amount of water (up to 5,000 gallons) in a tank once situated behind the wall.

The elaborately nailed baize door in the Staircase Hall leads to the North Corridor and the servants' quarters in the basement. The original was destroyed in the fire

THE BASEMENT

The basement was the 'engine-room' of a big house. Here, the servants prepared and stored the food and drink, cleaned the dishes, glasses and cutlery, kept the linen for the Dining Room and bedrooms, trimmed the lamps, and maintained supplies of housekeeping equipment. It was also where they dined. Uppark had both a Steward's Hall (for the upper servants) and a Servants' Hall. The butler and housekeeper had their own rooms from 1704, as befitted their superior status as heads of department with responsibility for the male and female servants respectively. The butler (and previously the steward) was the head of the household.

As well as performing routine duties (cleaning, laying fires, etc.), the servants were summoned at other times by means of a comprehensive system of bells which rang in the basement passage. Two staircases linked the below-stairs world with that of the family, and with the servants' bedrooms in the attic. After *c*.1815, underground tunnels communicated with the separate stable block to the west

(for coaches, carts and hunting, the three equestrian departments since 1704; the grooms slept above the stables) and with the Kitchen and Laundry block to the east. The tunnels also linked the house with the Dairy and the other various estate offices, which were laid out behind the stable block (see p.92). The functional efficiency of the basement depended on good communications with the group of buildings surrounding the house. The basement rooms have been refurnished since the fire in accordance, as closely as possible, with the recently discovered inventory of 1874.

THE STILL ROOM (KITCHEN)

This was the site of the original Uppark kitchen, which was placed in the basement in accordance with the practice recommended by Restoration architects like Roger Pratt. Around 1815 Sir Harry constructed a new kitchen in Paine's eastern service

*The Kitchen
before the
fire*

block, again in line with contemporary opinion, which was more concerned about fire and smells than the convenience of servants. Between *c.*1815 and *c.*1895, when the Kitchen was returned here, this was probably the Still Room, where cakes and preserves would have been made. It was also where coffee and tea would have been prepared and would have been used to make final touches to food *en route* from the Kitchen to the Servery. It doubled as a china store and a sitting-room for the housekeeper and the Still Room maids.

The room survived the fire relatively unscathed, although the ceiling had to be replaced due to water damage. Much of the paintwork has been left as it was before the fire.

PAST FURNISHINGS

The early eighteenth-century inventories list the contents of the room in great detail. In 1722, for example, it contained:

A large Range and Iron Back, a pair of Spitt Racks, four Spitts, two Iron Dripping panns and frames, a

Gridiron, three Trevetts, a Jack compleat, a Shovell, Tongs, Poker and two fenders, a copper Boyler, a large Kettle, a pottage pott and cover, a Stew pan, a Small Copper and iron work fixt, a large loose Copper.

Their value was the not inconsiderable sum of £13 3s.

The 1874 inventory of the Still Room lists a mahogany bookcase and '10 rush seated chairs', together with a wealth of equipment for jam and pastry making.

PRESENT FURNISHINGS

The open kitchen range installed *c.*1895 by Col. Turnour-Fetherstonhaugh, the large oak kitchen table, and the shelves holding the remnants of the *batterie de cuisine* (in 1874 there were '34 copper saucepans') recall the cooking facilities of a century ago. The 'New Gold Medal Eagle Range' supplied by the Eagle Range and Grate Co. of 127 Regent Street, London, allowed (as the inscriptions reveal) for all forms of cooking: baking, roasting (in the oven, and against the grill in front), boiling and keeping food warm. A ventilator system evacuated the fumes.

Against the side wall is an early nineteenth-century brick stewing stove. It was fired by charcoal, which provided a constant heat for the preparation of stews, sauces and preserves.

THE SCULLERY

Here the cutlery, crockery and glassware were washed. The plates were dried above the sink in racks made of wood to reduce the risk of accidental breakage. The late eighteenth-century oven suggests that this may have doubled as a pastry room.

THE BUTLER'S PANTRY

It is possible that this has always been the butler's sanctum; the 1705 inventory lists a 'Butler's Room' in what could have been the same position. This is an early reference to a figure who was to become pre-eminent only in the nineteenth century.

As head of the male servants (footmen and hall-boys, for example), the butler was responsible for waiting upon the master and his guests, for the serving of wine, food, coffee and tea, and for laying the table in the Dining Room. He also kept the silver and glassware clean, and maintained the wine cellar and the supplies of other liquids, including drinking water. A gauge above the fireplace used to record the water level in the roof tanks, and an Edwardian water filter, supplied by the Berkefeld Filter Co. Ltd, London, is still attached above the sink. Depending on the size of the household, the butler might also be responsible for the care of the master's clothes, though at Uppark in Sir Harry's time and previously, this was the duty of the valet. In the days before electricity, lamps and candles were also within the butler's domain.

Wells's fictional portrayal of a butler's pantry in *Tono-Bungay* was based on his experiences at Uppark. He described 'footmen and Rabbits [the butler] and estate men of all sorts among the green baize and Windsor chairs of the pantry – where Rabbits, being above the law, sold beer without a licence or any compunction.'

The butler, Thomas Deller, who was 50 years in Sir Harry's service; drawing by C. H. Tatham, 1806

PAST FURNISHINGS

In 1705 there were the usual paraphernalia of the butler's craft, including a bottle rack, '2 Crewets', dozens of bottles, glasses and knives, as well as a 'Block to wigs', which was used as a stand for the master's wig and perhaps also for his own in idler moments. In 1874 the picture was remarkably similar: glasses for water, champagne, claret, hock, sherry and liqueurs; wine coolers, decanters, carafes and bottles; 'champagne nippers', a lever corkscrew (possibly one attached to a table); sundry cleaning utensils including two sets of blacking brushes (for shoes), fourteen plate brushes (for silver) and three clothes brushes; numerous candlesticks and snuffers as well as 'about 16 lbs wax candles'.

In order to keep track of all this, the butler was provided with a 'Mahogany Escritoire with book-case top' and a 'China inkstand'. To keep him comfortable, there was a 'foot warmer' as well as, of course, fire irons to mind the fire. He could even sleep here in a 'Press bedstead' with a wool mattress, bolster and pillow, but the bed was probably intended for a footman, when on duty at night. Apart from the desk, the furnishings included several chairs, a mahogany round table, a three-fold fire-screen, an 'airing horse' to dry cloths, and a deal table. The walls were decorated with '5 coloured prints', a 'Buck's head' and a pair of horns.

PRESENT FURNISHINGS

The Pantry has again been laid out with the advice of a professional butler, Arthur Inch, to ensure authenticity. The room has been redecorated in the cream and brown livery found in several basement rooms. However, in the nineteenth century and previously the room was painted in soft distemper in a series of bright colours: pink, green, ultramarine and yellow.

Giving off the Butler's Pantry are two rooms.

THE SAFE

This is lined with slate shelves for the storage of plate and other valuables. The butler was traditionally responsible for the security of the silver.

To the left:

'THE LAMP ROOM'

This is shown as the Lamp Room, although its location (by 1882) was in a larger room (not on show) opposite the door to the Beer Cellar. The original use of this room is unknown. The 1874 inventory reveals that the Lamp Room, the main purpose of which was the preparation of lamps for lighting the house, contained 'Reading candles', 'Passage' and 'Victor' lamps and '6 Argand lamps' (which were recommended by Repton for the Servery, see p.49) as well as a 'trimming can' (for the oil), and a table and stool to make their maintenance here comfortable.

In the passage outside the door to the Butler's Pantry is a water filter in the form of a tree trunk inscribed: 'Spongy iron Filter Bischofs Patents No.5'.

THE HOUSEKEEPER'S ROOM

The housekeeper is always portrayed with a bunch of keys at her waist, denoting her responsibility for running the household. The female servants looked to her for direction in their housekeeping duties: laying fires, dusting, cleaning, making beds, waiting upon female members of the family and guests. The housekeeper also looked after the Still Room and regulated the household expenses for general supplies and for the kitchen laundry. This was the chief failing of Wells's mother Sarah, who was housekeeper at Uppark in the late nineteenth century (see p.30):

She did not know how to plan work, control servants, buy stores or economize in any way. She did not know clearly what was wanted upstairs. She could not even add up her accounts with assurance and kept them for me to do for her.

In *Tono-Bungay* Wells precisely described this room:

The much cupboarded, white-painted, chintz-brightened housekeeper's room where the upper servants assembled [and where] there was an old peerage and a Crockford together with the books of recipes, the *Whitaker's Almanack*, the *Old Moore's Almanack*, and the eighteenth-century dictionary, on the little dresser that broke the cupboards on one side of my mother's room.

The Housekeeper's Room was also the non-fictional scene of an entertainment devised by the young Wells one winter when:

a great snowstorm snowed me up for nearly a fortnight and I produced a daily newspaper of a facetious character, *The Up Park Alarmist* – on what was properly kitchen paper – and gave a shadow play to the maids and others, in a miniature theatre I made in the housekeeper's room.

PAST FURNISHINGS

The contents of this room were virtually identical in the lists of 1705 and 1722, comprising (in 1705): '1 press for the Linen, 1 Chest of Drawers, 1 Bin for Bred, 1 Chest for Candles, 2 Stores for Sweetmeats, 2 Tables, 8 Chaires, marbell mortar and pestle and preserving pan, 1 Looking Glass' and sundry equipment for the fire. A list of the linen reveals that it included sheets, pillowcases, damask table-cloths, napkins, lesser table-clothes for the 'Steward's

*The Housekeeper's
Room*

Table' and Servants' Hall, as well as '11 paire of Gentlemens Shirts', 'Towells' and 'Caloton [cotton?] Caps for my Lord'.

The 1874 inventory shows that the housekeeper's role had remained much the same. There was a great store of linen for both family and servants; tea-cups, plates, egg-cups, knives, forks, pickle jars, 'Sundry preserve jars', glasses, candlesticks, spirit measures, basins, jugs, sieves, flatirons and baskets in the 'Closet' or cupboard.

The furnishings were comfortable, including a two-fold screen, mahogany-framed chairs, a 'Round Claw table', a mahogany dining-table, an easy chair and a carpet and hearth rug. A barometer allowed the housekeeper's complaints about the weather to be up-to-date. 'Brass weights' enabled her to keep an eye on the allocation of spices and condiments; a clock and two engravings completed the furniture. There was a great emphasis on the taking of tea; a 'Tea kettle', 'Sundry teaware' and '6 Bread and butter plates' recall the scene described by Wells:

I hated tea-time in the Housekeeper's room more than anything else at Bladesover.... They sat about in black and shiny and flouncey clothing adorned with gimp and beads, eating great quantities of cake, drinking much tea in a stately manner and reverberating remarks. I remember these women as immense ... Tea lasted for nearly three-quarters of an hour ... and day after day the talk was exactly the same.

PRESENT FURNISHINGS

The room was severely damaged by the fire, as the floors above collapsed into it. None the less, the cupboards and woodwork remain substantially intact. The room has been repainted according to what is probably a pre-war scheme. The glazed dresser was originally painted grey and afterwards there were no fewer than fourteen coats of off-white (as described by Wells) before the colour was changed to pink.

CERAMICS

English blue-and-white plates and dishes, nineteenth-century, some Copeland.

A Caughley tea and coffee service, *c*.1790.

THE HOUSEKEEPER'S CLOSET

Before the fire, this was thought to have been the Still Room, but the 1874 inventory has revealed its proper name and use.

PAST CONTENTS

In 1705 it was where the housekeeper kept plates, tea and coffee pots, mugs, dessert glassware (such as 'Silleybub Glasses'), basins, a colander, wooden scales and weights, a coffee-mill and '13 Chamber pots'. In 1874 the contents were similar, but there were also preserve and pickle jars, and a lemon squeezer, as well as an ironing-board and flatirons.

THE BELL PASSAGE

Here a hall-boy would have waited to see which bell was ringing and where service was required. The appropriate servant would then have been summoned. There are two bell-boards.

NEARER HOUSEKEEPER'S ROOM:

The smaller board is of unusual design, a wooden box split into 14 flaps that fall open when the bell is activated. The handwritten labels inside indicate the source of the summons (and date the board between 1874 and 1893, although one room was still called 'Sir H[arry]'s Dressing Room').

BEYOND DOUBLE DOORS:

The large board is more conventional (and earlier in date, probably c.1800). After the bell had sounded, the pendulum beneath continued to swing to allow for the inattention of servants.

From the second half of the eighteenth century elaborate bell systems were installed. A complicated network of wires, joints and pulleys linked the bell-ropes in the rooms to the bells in the servants' passage. In 1836 William Summers, a London 'Stove Manufacturer' and plumber who was also installing a hot-air heating system at the time, billed Sir Harry for 'Repairing and partly new hanging the Bells throughout the house'. The system was no longer in working order by the time of the fire. Although it still does not work, all the fittings have been renovated since then and linked together with 'strong copper wire', as in 1836.

THE BEER AND WINE CELLARS

The columns and vaulting of the Beer Cellar suggest an earlier date than c.1690, but the remarkable similarity with the cellar at Stansted Park (also attributed to Talman, see p.13) indicates that this room does indeed belong to Lord Tankerville's rebuilding of Uppark. The room above (now the Saloon) was the 'Marble Hall' in 1705, and the vaults could have supported the weight of a marble floor. In 1706 there was both a 'Small beer Cellar' and a 'Strong beer Cellar', for the two different types of beer. The Small Beer Cellar was elsewhere, its location probably the same as in 1882, adjacent to the Steward's Hall.

The Wine Cellar, in 1882, was in the cellar giving off the Beer Cellar, and although the brick bins are unusual, their purpose was the storage of wine.

PAST CONTENTS

In 1706 there were '11 pipes Strong beer, 1 of them in bottles', as well as four full hogsheads, fourteen empty ones and '6 Iron screw'd Hoops' or barrels. There was an even greater amount of small beer. Beer at this time was a staple, which would have been brewed in the brew-house and drunk (even at breakfast) in the Servants' Hall. In 1874 the distinction between Small and Strong Beer Cellars persisted in the inventory; both cellars also contained brewing equipment such as a 'yeast skimmer', brewing tubs, tubing and a mallet (for the bungs). There were no less than 1,190 gallons of ale in what was then called the 'Ale Cellar'. Beer could be piped direct from the brew-house. The barrels and tubs described in the 1874 inventory have been reconstructed.

The 1874 inventory also mentions a Wine Cellar for the first time. This contained various liqueurs, brandies, gin, whisky, rum, sherry and other fortified wines, as well as burgundy and champagne.

THE STEWARD'S HALL

The original use of this room is unclear, although its size suggests that it may have been the Steward's Hall, listed in 1704, where the upper servants would have dined. From the nineteenth century these included the butler, under-butler, housekeeper, valet, head housemaid and lady's maid.

Similar halls (for example at Petworth or Ham House) were well furnished. At Uppark, the Steward's Hall or 'Parlor', as it was designated in 1705, contained '3 Tables' and '12 Black Chaires', and the contents were the same in 1722, when the chairs were described as old and 'Matted' (caned).

As at Petworth, the Uppark Steward's Room continued in use; the contents in 1874 included twelve mahogany chairs and one armchair placed around a circular mahogany table. Serving tables (of both deal and mahogany) accommodated knives, forks, plates (also for dessert), a 'Cruet stand and cruets' and ale glasses. With a Brussels carpet on the floor, seven oil paintings on the walls, a gilt chimney glass, porcelain on the chimneypiece, and a

sofa and armchairs, the Hall was a pleasant place to dine and to relax afterwards.

It is now also used as an exhibition room, whose principal treasure is the Uppark doll's-house, which is a microcosm of early eighteenth-century upstairs and downstairs country house life.

DOLL'S-HOUSE

It dates from c.1735–40 and was brought to Uppark by the marriage in 1746 of Sarah Lethieullier to Sir Matthew Fetherstonhaugh. The Lethieullier coat of arms is in the pediment. It is one of the two most important eighteenth-century British doll's-houses and is in a remarkable state of preservation, being

The Dining Room in the Uppark doll's-house

only slightly damaged by its hurried evacuation from the house in 1989. The doll's-house at Nostell Priory, Yorkshire (also National Trust), attributed to Thomas Chippendale, is remarkably similar.

Both houses consist of three floors standing on a rusticated basement. The pedimented façades, in Palladian style, are both surmounted by a balustrade supporting statues; they open to reveal interiors below and above stairs, thus giving a rare insight into rooms that have never changed, immune from the alterations that are made in real country houses. In the Upark doll's-house, every detail is minutely accurate, from the pictures, which are individually painted in oil, to the silver, which is real and hallmarked, although not dated. It would therefore have been intended not only as a plaything, but also as an amusement for adults. Indeed, its excellent state of preservation suggests that the children of the Lethieullier and Fetherstonhaugh families must have been closely supervised. In *Tono-Bungay*, Wells wrote of playing 'discreetly' with the 'great doll's house . . . under imperious direction'.

IN CENTRE OF BOTTOM FLOOR:

THE STAIRCASE HALL

It is furnished as an upper servants' dining-room with contents reminiscent of those in the Steward's Hall (see p.82). The cabriole-legged, leather-upholstered chairs, the black lacquer longcase clock and the landscape glass are all of *c*.1720 in design. The brass sconces on either side of the fireplace are complete with their overhanging glass smoke shades, as a protection against the staining of the ceiling. A wooden-headed servant in livery stands beside a gate-leg table set for tea.

TO LEFT:

THE KITCHEN

It is superbly equipped with pewter plates, decoratively arranged in two tiers of shelving, pots and pans, a mortar and pestle (for pounding spices), and a flatiron. Out-of-scale coffee pots and (to the right) a chocolate-maker stand on the floor, while a Leedsware white coffee/chocolate pot is ready on the table. There is a generous supply of ivory knives and forks. Racks for a spit hang above the fireplace. The cook is dressed in printed cotton protected by a full-length pinafore.

TO RIGHT:

THE HOUSEKEEPER'S ROOM

It is a plain apartment with good quality mahogany furniture and expensive mirrors. A real housekeeper's room would have contained numerous functional items in cupboards within the room and in an adjoining closet (see p.80), Here, however, the housekeeper sits in her best apron awaiting her guests. The tea-table, tea-caddy, sugar bowl and cups and saucers are possibly the most complete set of its kind. On the marble-topped side-table is a collection of glassware.

THE DRAWING ROOM

Upstairs, the rooms are more lofty, befitting their higher status. In the Drawing Room (to the left) the family sits at tea around a silver table with matching teapot and tea things. A needlework carpet, silver sconces (again, with glass smoke shades above), a giltwood mirror and the richly carved furniture, upholstered in silk, indicate that this is the principal floor of the house. On this floor and above are the doll family's collection of pictures; sparsely hung, as in most English houses of the time, over doors and chimneys (always with a glass beneath, as in the real Upark). Their collection is unusual in containing only landscapes (mainly seventeenth-century Flemish in style); there are none of the more usual English portraits. On the upper floors, the doors are painted green, and have large brass rim locks. At the windows are festoon silk curtains, which were restored, as in the real house, by Lady Meade-Fetherstonhaugh in the 1930s. The dolls (made of wax rather than the wood used for the servants) are richly dressed, the ladies wearing the pannier silk skirts, supported by hooped undergarments, that were fashionable around 1730.

THE DINING ROOM

The dining-room was often placed centrally in seventeenth- and early eighteenth-century houses. The centrepiece is a blue japanned buffet with shelves for the display of silver and gold. The sole occupants are a *blanc-de-Chine* monkey and two liveried footmen. In the foreground are several outsize silver items including a two-handled porringer and a monteith (or glass cooler), both *c*.1690 in style.

THE PRINCIPAL BEDROOM

The grandest bedrooms were to be found on the main floor until the end of the eighteenth century. Here, and upstairs, the silk-hung beds, *c*.1715–20 in style, are of 'flying' or 'angel' type, the canopy being supported by a hook in the ceiling rather than by posts. The lady of the house is lying in after the birth of twins, who are sleeping in a wicker cradle, watched attentively by their nurse. The seat furniture is made of ivory, a very unusual and highly expensive commodity, usually found in furniture imported from India, although these chairs are entirely English in style. The dressing-table, covered in lace, is provided with a gilt mirror. The bedwarmer has a turned ebony handle.

THE TOP-FLOOR BEDROOMS

The grandest bedroom is in the centre, with a gold silk bed flanked by doors, all four of which have overdoor pictures. Again, the furniture is of ivory; the right-hand bedroom is provided with an ivory-inlaid ebony chest on a stand supporting a garniture of seventeenth-century Chinese blue-and-white porcelain. China jars also stand in the fireplaces in typical early eighteenth-centuy style. Each bedroom has its dressing-table and mirrors, there are fire-irons to mind the fire, and sconces illuminate the comfortably furnished interiors.

THE SERVANTS' HALL

This was where the lower servants took their meals, seated in strict order of precedence. The juniors would have sat nearest the door (where the draughts were greatest, although the proximity to the fire would have been a consolation). There would also have been strict rules about behaviour, as recorded, for example, by the eighteenth-century 'Servants' Rules' boards that still survive in houses like Clandon.

Wells wrote: 'Up Park below stairs was gay at Christmas and I was gay with it.' One has to imagine these special holidays with the Servants' Hall *en fête*, as well as the daily round of breakfasts, lunches and dinners.

PAST FURNISHINGS

In 1704 the Servants' Hall contained '1 Table, 2 fformes, a gt cubbord, 1 little table'. The same table and forms were still there in 1874, and another table was used to store the knives, forks and spoons. Plates were warmed by a 'Japanned plate warmer', and there was a butler's tray to carry food from the Kitchen. The decorations were limited to nine pairs of bucks' horns and an oil painting. In a cupboard near the Hall were kept copper jugs, trays, candlesticks and a bread tray.

THE SUBTERRANEAN PASSAGES

From the basement, visitors proceed along the central passage past coal and wood stores to a 'T' junction. To the left is the way to the western pavilion, which was probably built by Paine *c*.1750 and contains the stables, and (no access) to the brewhouse courtyard and the other estate buildings. To the right, the passage leads to the eastern pavilion, which in *c*.1750 combined a greenhouse and laundry and to which Sir Harry moved the kitchen *c*.1815. It now houses the restaurant and shop.

One of the underground passages in 1941

CHAPTER EIGHT
THE GARDEN, PARK AND ESTATE

'It would appear presumptive in me, to suggest any improvement or alteration to a place which possesses so many natural advantages as Uppark,' wrote Humphry Repton in the preamble to his Red Book of 1810. He described as 'truely magnificent' its site 'on the summit of the south down range of hills', its 'large masses of wood, the beautiful shapes and verdure of the lawns, with the distant and various views of Sea and Sand'. The earliest view of the house, engraved by Johannes Kip and published in 1707, shows the surrounding woods opened up to the south to reveal the Solent and the Isle of Wight.

In 1695 Celia Fiennes found the 'new built house' within a 'very fine Parke' with 'stately woods and shady tall trees at least two mile. . . . Its in the midst of fine gardens, gravell and grass walks and bowling green, with breast walls divideing each from other. . . . it looks very neate and all orchards and yards convenient'. Her account confirms both the essential veracity of Kip's engraving and that the house built by Lord Tankerville c.1690 stood in an established woodland setting. The formal gardens were typical of the time. They comprised walled enclosures laid out on either side of the principal approach to the house, which was from the east through a wooded avenue and the two service blocks. The planting seems to have consisted of rectangular parterrres of low, clipped hedges and standard bushes. A terrace to the south of the house and parallel with the main approach provided another vista through a gate-screen and woodland to the sea, and views over the open parkland to the south, as today. If William Talman designed the house, it is possible that the royal gardener George London supplied designs for the garden. Talman and London collaborated at Hampton Court Palace after 1689 and at Dyrham Park, Gloucestershire (also National Trust), where London was employed

from 1691. London also laid out the formal gardens at Petworth after c.1693.

In 1706 the garden tools at Uppark included 'garden Shears', an 'Edgeing Iron', a 'Cutting Iron', shovels, rakes, a 'Levill', wheelbarrows and 'Stone Rowlers' (for flattening the turf). '9 pare of bowles one Jak' were for the bowling green, which Kip shows in use to the south-west of the house. There were also numerous wooden tubs, flowerpots and 'watering pots'.

The next two views of Uppark were painted before 1734 by Pieter Tillemans. They show that the formal gardens depicted by Kip had already disappeared, apart from a walled enclosure behind the house. The two service and stable blocks to the east were still in the same position but had been considerably altered (possibly 1723–5). In front of the house was a large round pond. This does not appear to have lasted long, and being high on a chalk hill, would probably have dried out in the summer, but its outlines can still be discerned from the air in dry weather. With the terraces removed, cattle were free to roam up to the windows of the house. Thick woods still encompassed the house on three sides.

Samuel Hieronymus Grimm's watercolour of 1782 again shows the house with its surrounding woods, the parkland open to the south. To the north-east, one of the present flanking pavilions appears. This and its pendant stable block to the west are attributed to James Paine (c.1750), who demolished the earlier pair of buildings in the process, at the behest of Sir Matthew Fetherstonhaugh, who must also have commissioned a plan (c.1750) of the gardens. This plan has been tentatively attributed to 'Capability' Brown, who practised as a consulting landscape gardener after 1749 and occasionally beforehand, while employed at Stowe in Buckinghamshire. With its serpentine walks winding between various points of interest, it is reminiscent of Brown's embellishment of the existing Pleasure Ground at Petworth in 1751–7. But it is unclear whether the 'Menagery', the 'Rotundo upon the Great Mount' or the circular pond or 'Bason' described on the plan ever existed. The Trust's recent replanting of the garden behind Paine's eastern pavilion with shrubs and plants available in the eighteenth and early nineteenth centuries does, however, make quotations from the plan, and Repton noted an existing 'Flower Garden' in this location. The *c.*1750 plan describes the eastern pavilion as a 'Greenhouse and Laundry'. It was called the 'Greenhouse Wing' on Repton's plan, and housed from *c.*1815 a kitchen from which food was brought underground to the house. Entries in Sir Matthew's Account Book for 1748 record gardening expenses which tally with the plan attributed to Brown, eg 'To ye Menagerie for the Mans Wages

4.7.6' and 'To Francis Ruddall on acct., of Pond makg.... 11.6.11'. Sir Matthew bought orange trees in 1748, 1765 and 1767. Between 1766 and 1767 he paid nearly £200 'in Labour Work in the Garden'. However, apart from the mysterious plan, there is little to indicate what he actually achieved, although, in 1768 he lamented the loss of 'Wall Trees' in his 'new garden'.

In 1746 the value of the timber in the park was said to be equivalent to the £19,000 paid by Sir Matthew for the whole estate. The sale map shows the surviving walled kitchen garden to the east of the main house, indicating that it was built before 1746. In 1748 Sir Matthew planted chestnut and walnut trees. He stocked the park with red deer and maintained the park palings of riven oak. Venison, pheasant and turtle (where were they kept?) were despatched to his political patron, the Duke of Newcastle. Sir Matthew extended his landholdings

View over the Downs towards South Harting in the early eighteenth century; by Pieter Tillemans (Staircase Hall)

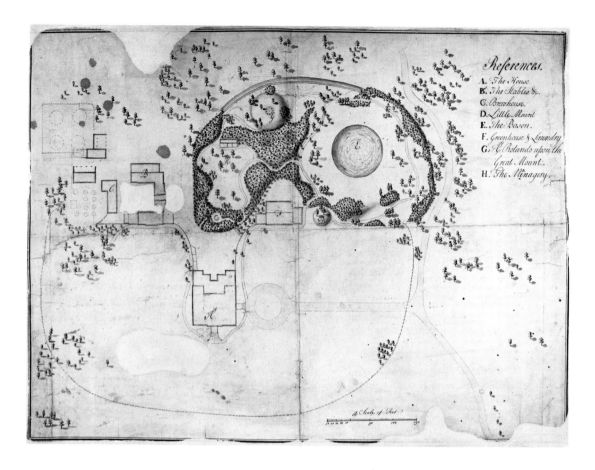

The mid-eighteenth-century plan of the garden, attributed to 'Capability' Brown

by purchasing local estates. In 1755 he began the purchase of lands near Harting, belonging to the Catholic Caryll family. This was a long drawn-out process that was completed by the acquisition of the adjoining Lady Holt estate in 1767. In 1769 Sir Matthew invested in the American Grand Ohio Company, which sought to develop lands bought from the local population by the creation of a colony to be called Vandalia. By tradition, the ruinous banqueting house in the park to the north of Uppark, built by Henry Keene, is called the Vandalian Tower, but it is more likely that it was erected in celebration of Harry's coming-of-age in 1775, although it was not completed until 1776. The Vandalian scheme failed on the outbreak of war with the American colonies in 1775.

Good husbandry continued after Sir Matthew's death in 1774. The record of his widow's annual expenditure included items such as:

'The labour for mowing the parks, and sundries £18.17.4'.
'She bought 25 quarters of beans for the deer £39.0.0'.

About 50 workers lived in cottages on the estate. Sixteen men maintained the woods and fences. Shepherds tended their flocks on the downs. Sarah, Lady Fetherstonhaugh's niece, Elizabeth Iremonger, described the beauty of Uppark at harvest-time in 1786:

This Country has always peculiar Charms; there is nothing like it and I am always sorry to quit it. We enjoyed the few hot Days and evenings during the last Moon very much; my Aunt and I frequently drove in the Harvest-fields by moonlight, in an open Carriage, and supped at our return by the same light, without

Candles. Perhaps You did not suspect I was such a Lunatick.

Sir Harry appears to have been less of a countryman than his father, despite his opinion that 'there is no pursuit affording more rational amusement or more solid advantages in country retirement than in the management of a farm'. His friends included famous agricultural improvers such as the 3rd Earl of Egremont and the 5th and 6th Dukes of Bedford. Freely admitting his indolence and a tendency to lounge when in the country, Sir Harry was nevertheless a passionate sportsman. He took an interest in the minutiae of shooting, arranging grand *battues* for his friends but also enjoying 'hedge-row shooting in autumn'. Repton probably designed for him the detached Game Larder by the north drive (see p.90).

Repton probably came to Sir Harry's notice either through the Prince of Wales (see p.28) or through John Russell, 6th Duke of Bedford, for whom Repton produced the Woburn Red Book in 1804. Repton's principal recommendation was the construction of a new northern entrance to Uppark (see p.90). This also entailed a drive from the South Harting lodge leading through woodland via a new set of 'golden gates' and thence to an avenue that framed his Tuscan portico. Repton's concept has been restored since the 1989 fire. However, two of Repton's grandest proposals remained on paper, possibly due to Sir Harry's need to economise. It is probably for this reason that the Red Book was designed so 'that a part may be executed without carrying the whole into effect . . . so as to compleat the place whenever it is thought adviseable'.

Although he was enthusiastic about the natural beauty of Uppark, Repton felt that the house appeared too small from a distance, due to its isolation from the flanking pavilions. This made it look like 'the shooting box of a Woodland Country, than the Palace worthy of so proved a situation'.

Repton's proposal for the entrance drive from his Red Book of 1810

He proposed linking the buildings by colonnades to create the impression of a much larger house (as Wyatt and Bonomi had done at nearby Stansted Park between 1786 and 1791). Repton also wished to separate the house from the park on the grounds that an 'architectural terrace and balustrade would be more appropriate than mere grass slopes without any defence from the intrusion of beasts and cattle'. Although the terrace was never built, a fence enclosing shrubs surrounded the house in Neale's engraving of 1821, and this could explain Repton's praise in 1815 of Uppark's 'olfactory joy' – 'every room has its depot of odours for permanent use – while every window has its Orange tree and Tube roses – and admits perfume from the surrounding beds of Mignionette and Heliotrope – till the whole is an atmosphere of sweets'. Repton also advised on the flower garden, suggesting a parterre 'in which the flints and rock plants are proposed to prevail' and, by contrast, 'a whimsical arrangement of plants made by Linnaeus in such order that a dial or clock was produced by the time of opening and shutting of certain flowers'. This proved impossible, but there is a Repton drawing of a flower garden with pavilions and a clock-shaped bed. (Lady Meade-Fetherstonhaugh remade the 'Sundial Bed' in 1933.)

The Uppark estate was handed on 'intact and well maintained' by Sir Harry's widow and her sister. In 1851 203 workers were employed on the 5,000-acre estate. Comparison of the 1746 and 1880 maps shows that the extent of the deer-park was very much the same (336 acres in 1746). Their successor, Col. Turnour-Fetherstonhaugh, preserved the old traditions and 'only bought cows and bred them from the original [Guernsey] herd he inherited when he first came to Uppark'. After his death, Lady Meade-Fetherstonhaugh regretted the sale in 1931 of the farm horses, implements and carts. By the 1930s, the garden was overgrown (including what may have been Repton's dial and rock gardens), and the Meade-Fetherstonhaughs undertook much clearing and replanting as well as removing creepers from the west and east fronts of the house. The wider landscape remained essentially as it had for over 200 years. The house still retained its surrounding woodland, and Repton's avenue (replanted since 1989) beyond the golden gates

required only 'cutting branches, etc.'. It was not until the 1960s that arable farming broke up the old parkland into small enclosures, thus marking the end of Uppark's medieval deer-park. In addition, the storms of 1987 and 1990 felled old trees in the park and in the woods to the north and west of the house. Replanting has been carried out by both the Meade-Fetherstonhaugh family and the Trust. It is to be hoped that regeneration of forest and park trees will eventually restore the former grandeur of the Uppark landscape.

TOUR OF THE GARDEN

The area immediately to the north of the garden was once densely planted with beech trees, which provided an appropriate backdrop to views of the house from the south. The car-park has been moved further from the house so that a mixture of broad-leaved species can be reinstated here.

THE ENTRANCE DRIVE

The garden is enclosed on the north, west and east sides by a wall of knapped flint that first appears on the mid-eighteenth-century map attributed to 'Capability' Brown. In creating his new north approach to the house, Repton pierced the garden wall with a new gateway known as the 'golden gates'. He recommended topping the gate-piers with sphinxes or lions, but neither seems to have been added. In the 1880s the piers had large ball finials on which the Uppark peacocks were fond of roosting (both now gone).

Repton's formal north drive, linking the gates with his new entrance portico, has been replanted since the fire with Norway maples (*Acer platanoïdes*).

Turn left (east) off the entrance drive to reach the Game Larder.

THE GAME LARDER

This charming little flint-walled building does not appear on Repton's plan of the buildings existing in 1810. It is therefore probable that he designed it;

The Game Larder

he certainly made suggestions for the decorative arrangement of dead game within it.

The Game Larder, which was sited well away from the house because of the smell, consists of two rooms. The first is entered through a door framed with circular air vents. It is octagonal and paved with contrasting stone and slate slabs. Game (here mainly birds) was hung to ripen from iron hooks in the ceiling (arranged in a star shape, according to Repton's drawing) and was originally protected from flies by finely perforated metal sheets fitted into the large windows, which would have provided the necessary through draught. The second, rectangular room was used for hanging venison and larger carcases. The path to the north is of pebble setts framed by squares of deer vertebrae.

Beyond the Game Larder to the east is the east service block.

THE EAST SERVICE BLOCK

Balancing the stable block to the north-west of the main house, the eastern service block was probably designed by James Paine *c.*1750. The bell is dated 1754. On a contemporary garden plan, this building (now the restaurant and shop) was described as a

'Greenhouse and laundry', and Repton's Red Book (1810) called it the 'Greenhouse Wing'. The green-house would have been in the front of the building (the present restaurant), to take advantage of the southerly aspect, and would have been warmed in winter by the stoves of the Laundry behind. In *c.*1815 Sir Harry decided to convert the greenhouse into a kitchen – hence the cast-iron range at the west end. Food was carried through the tunnel and up the stairs to the Servery. After 1895, when the Kitchen returned to the house, it was left empty, and the windows bricked up.

PAST FURNISHINGS

In 1874 the Kitchen was amply supplied with furniture and equipment including a deal dresser, china cupboard, six Windsor chairs, bread and flour bins, pans and kettles for meat and fish cookery, a pestle and mortar, several chopping blocks, a 'Weighing machine' and numerous knives, choppers, skewers and ladles. The room was lit by a '4 light Argand Lamp', and there was also an '8 Day clock', probably the clock still here. There was also a larder (presumably one of the adjoining rooms), which contained reserve equipment and, incongruously, a 'Washing Tub', perhaps belonging to the Laundry (which was situated in the back of the building). In 1874 the Laundry contained various tubs, a 'Scrubbing horse', a 'Patent mangle' to squeeze water out of wet clothes, 'Drying racks' to dry them and an 'Ironing stove & piping' together with fifteen flatirons. Repton's 1810 plan shows the 'Linen Yard' (where laundry would have been left to dry in the sun) to the north-west of the house. He recommended moving it closer to the Laundry.

Adjoining the East Service Block to the east is the Gothick Seat.

THE GOTHICK SEAT

It was probably commissioned by Sir Matthew *c.*1760, perhaps from Henry Keene, who later built the Gothick Vandalian Tower (see p.88). The original colour is unknown, but this may have been the 'Summer Seat' that was grained and varnished 'as before' in 1862. Sir Matthew's Account Book for

1758 notes: 'To Miller [Sir Matthew's clerk of works] Gothick seats at Uppark £70 19s 7d'. In 1760 John Banks was paid £25 'for the seat'. These are considerable sums, even for the elaborate vaulted structure that survives today.

Beside the Gothick Seat is a planting of the *Saponaria officinalis* which Lady Meade-Fetherstonhaugh used to clean the Uppark textiles (see p.36).

Behind the East Service Block and Gothick Seat is the Amphitheatre Garden.

THE AMPHITHEATRE GARDEN

This is an open glade surrounded by shrubs and trees, which have been depleted by the recent storms. The Trust is replanting this area in an informal, 'Brownian' style with serpentine walks, mainly evergreen shrubs such as box and yew around the lawn and as a backdrop to the Coade stone urn.

'THE URN ON THE MOUNT'

So called by Repton, who probably installed it here as an eye-catcher on his northern approach. The urn is a two-thirds-size copy of the Borghese Vase, one of the most celebrated of Greek antiquities which was at the Villa Borghese, Rome by 1645, and is now in the Louvre. The Uppark copy of *c*.1800 is made of Coade stone, an artificial material named after Eleanor Coade, whose factory at Lambeth produced a wide variety of sculpture and architectural ornament. The mount on which it stands dates back to at least the mid-eighteenth century.

Cross the Entrance Drive to the western side of the garden.

THE STABLES

The western pavilion, also probably by Paine *c*.1750, was built as a stable block incorporating the '7 Stall Stable' (open to visitors) mentioned in 1874, when it contained horse cloths, halters and other equine equipment, as well as straw and a 'Stable barrow'. In 1874 and presumably earlier, there were also a 'Cart Stable' for cart horses, two coach-houses

containing carriages, and 'Carriage Stables' for carriage horses. A 'Harness Room' contained halters, saddles and bridles, which would have been cleaned there. Around the stable courtyard (open to view but not access) there were various estate buildings, including the brew-house. Here, and in the adjoining timber and wood yards, were ranged the buildings fundamental to the operation of the house and estate. These include carpenter's and blacksmith's shops, a tool house, a stone-mason's shed, a hog house and slaughter house. There were also extensive garden sheds and greenhouses containing plants and equipment.

In the borders along the west terrace are grown three types of lavender – English, 'Twickel Purple' and 'Hidcote'.

At the western end of the west terrace is the Dairy.

THE DAIRY

Tinged with the curiosity of Sir Harry's romance with his dairymaid (whom he married in 1825), this little building has been the subject of much speculation. According to *Uppark and its People*:

One day, as Sir Harry sauntered on the grass terrace, he caught the sound of a girl's voice singing. He asked the Housekeeper who was the girl whose voice had attracted him so much. 'Not the Dairymaid, Sir Harry, she be too old –', was the reply. Sir Harry continued to listen to the voice that charmed him. The Dairymaid had helpers; one day, when the noise of angry voices was heard as he approached the Dairy, he heard a girl's voice saying, 'Peace, peace . . .'; and there was peace. The old Dairymaid retired, and the girl who cried 'Peace, peace . . .' was established as head of the Dairy with a handful of girls at her command. Her name was Mary Ann Bullock.

. . . One day, Sir Harry presented himself at the door of the Dairy. He told Mary Ann he wanted to marry her. In an account, never to be forgotten, of the episode told by a later Dairymaid who had heard the story from contemporaries, Mary Ann was said to be speechless; 'taken aback like . . .'. 'Don't answer me now,' said Sir Harry, 'but if you will have me, cut a slice out of the leg of Mutton that is coming up for my dinner today . . .' When the Mutton arrived, the slice was cut.

The Dairy

In the 1880s, the dairymaid was Kenturah Denning, who had to get up at 3am to make 'fresh butter and Devonshire cream, cream cheese, butter pats and other butter all sorts of fancy shapes, to decorate the breakfast table'. She was also required to serve tea in the Dairy with 'junket, Devonshire cream and fruit'.

Oddly for a building that needed to be kept cool, the Dairy faces south. (Ice came from one of the two ice-houses, ruins of which survive in Garden Wood near the old ice pond.) The Dairy can be dated to *c*.1800, although it may have been built by Repton after *c*.1810. The interior was renovated in 1832, when the stained glass and the white glazed tiles 'with rich Enamelled Flower Border' were installed by the London decorator Charles Pepper.

PAST FURNISHINGS

The 1874 inventory lists the contents of both the 'Inner Dairy' and the 'Old Dairy'. The former contained a 'Marble top table [*in situ*], 21 milk pans, 7 cream crocks, 3 milking pails, skimmer, churn stand . . . scales and weights, Butter Tray and board'. There were also 'sundry prints', presumably decorative butter moulds.

PRESENT FURNISHINGS

The 'Old Dairy' retains its pump, fireplace and copper. The sloping wooden gutter directed water from the pump into the copper in which it would be heated. Hot water was used for washing utensils, scalding cream (to make clotted cream) or warming milk for cheese-making.

THE SOUTH TERRACES

The grass terraces which run parallel with the south front of the house date back at least to the early eighteenth century. They provide superb views over the former deer-park and the valley to the south.

BIBLIOGRAPHY

The Tankerville papers relating to Uppark, Chillingham Castle and Dawley are mainly deposited in the Essex and Northumberland Record Offices in Chelmsford and Newcastle, and in the Public Record Office in London. The records of Fetherstone Castle are in the Northumberland Record Office. The principal Fetherstonhaugh and Lethieullier archive is on deposit in the West Sussex Record Office in Chichester, together with various maps and wills, and Repton's Red Book. The documents retained in the house were destroyed by the fire. Mrs Wells's diaries are in the Rare Book and Special Collections Library of the University of Illinois at Urbana-Champaign.

ALDSWORTH, F.G., 'An Eighteenth-century Gothic Folly at Uppark', *Sussex Archaeological Collections*, cxxi, 1983, pp.215–19.

ALLNUT, Alan, and EYRE, John, 'Water supply to Uppark', *Sussex Industrial History*, xv, 1985/6.

ANON., 'Uppark', *Country Life*, xxvii, 1910, p.702.

ANON., 'Chillingham Castle', *Country Life*, xxxiii, 8 March 1913, pp.346–55.

ANON., 'Uppark', *Antique Collector*, December 1952, pp.238–46.

ASLET, Clive, 'Stansted Park I, II and III', *Country Life*, clxxi, 1982, pp.346, 410, 478.

COBBETT, William, *Complete Collection of State Trials*, ix, 1811, pp.127–86.

COLERIDGE, Anthony, 'Don Petro's Table Tops: Scagliola and Grand Tour Clients', *Apollo*, lxxxiii, March 1966, pp.184–7.

COLERIDGE, Anthony, 'Georgian Cabinet Makers at Uppark', *Connoisseur*, October, November 1967.

CORNFORTH, John, 'Featherstone Castle', *Country Life*, cliv, 25 October 1973, pp.1246–9.

CRUIKSHANK, Dan, 'Rebuilding Uppark', *Country Life*, 18 January 1990, pp.56–7.

DALLAWAY, James, *A History of the Western Division of the County of Sussex*, 1815.

EYRE, John, 'A Sequence of Letters between Sir Matthew Fetherstonhaugh Bart and Thomas First Duke of Newcastle', *West Sussex History*, 54, October 1994, pp.2–13; 55, April 1995, pp.10–20.

GORDON, H.D., *The History of Harting*, 1877.

GORE, St John, 'A Grand Tour Collection', *Country Life*, 2 December 1965.

GREY, Ford, Lord, *The Secret History of the Rye-House Plot: and of Monmouth's Rebellion*, 1754.

HODGSON, John, *The History of Northumberland*, 1820–58.

HUSSEY, Christopher, 'Uppark I, II and III', *Country Life*, lxxxix, 1941, pp.520, 540, 562 (reprinted in *English Country Houses: Mid Georgian*, 1955, pp.29–40).

JENKINS, Rhys, 'A Chapter in the History of the Water Supply of London: A Thames-side Pumping Installation and Sir Edward Ford's Patent from Cromwell', *Transactions of the Newcomen Society*, ix, 1928/9 [1930], pp.43–51.

LEACH, Peter, *James Paine*, 1988.

LUMMIS, Trevor, and MARSH, Jan, *The Woman's Domain*, 1990, pp.119–44.

MEADE-FETHERSTONHAUGH, Margaret, and WARNER, Oliver, *Uppark and its People*, 1964; reprinted 1988, 1995.

NARES, Gordon, 'The Treasures of Uppark', *Country Life Annual*, 1956, pp.40–5.

NICOLSON, Adam, *The Fire at Uppark*, 1990.

PRICE, Cecil, *Cold Caleb: The Scandalous Life of Ford Grey, 1st Earl of Tankerville, 1655–1701*, 1956.

ROBINSON, John Martin, 'Rising from the Ashes', *Country Life*, 20 February 1992, pp.42–5.

TIPPING, H. Avray, *English Homes*, period IV, i, 1920, p.363.

WELLS, H.G., *Tono-Bungay*, 1908.

WELLS, H.G., *Experiment in Autobiography*, i, 1934.

WHITE, Roger, 'Conservation Issues in 1989–90: "Uppark", *Georgian Group Report and Journal*, 1989, pp.13–17.

WORSLEY, Giles, 'William Talman: Some Stylistic Suggestions', *Georgian Group Report and Journal*, 1992, pp.6–18.

INDEX